Self-Discipline

for
Entrepreneurs

How to Develop and Maintain

Self-Discipline as an

Entrepreneur

By

Martin Meadows

Download Another Book for Free

I want to thank you for buying my book and offer you another book (just as valuable as this book): *Grit: How to Keep Going When You Want to Give Up*, completely free.

Visit the link below to receive it:

http://www.profoundselfimprovement.com/selfdi sciplineforentrepreneurs

In *Grit*, I'll share with you exactly how to stick to your goals according to peak performers and scientific evidence.

In addition to getting *Grit*, you'll also have an opportunity to get my new books for free, enter giveaways, and receive other valuable emails from me.

Again, here's the link to sign up:

http://www.profoundselfimprovement.com/selfdi sciplineforentrepreneurs

Table of Contents

Prologue

As a person who has been self-employed his entire lifetime, I know how challenging entrepreneurship can be.

The difficulties people usually associate with working on your own—like finding a business idea, raising capital, creating your product, finding customers, and hiring employees—are only the start.

Entrepreneurship also poses challenges to your self-discipline. People who have never worked for themselves don't realize the rollercoaster self-employed people are on.

Self-discipline has been my forte ever since I was a young child. I still remember how I saved money instead of spending it like other kids, how I'd rather work on my long-term goals than party like other teenagers, how I stuck for years with every activity I liked instead of quitting them because of the first obstacles.

I've written two bestselling books about self-discipline – *How to Build Self-Discipline: Resist*

Temptations and Reach Your Long-Term Goals and *Daily Self-Discipline: Everyday Habits and Exercises to Build Self-Discipline and Achieve Your Goals*.

I'm also the author of a book about self-discipline for dieters – *Self-Disciplined Dieter: How to Lose Weight and Become Healthy Despite Cravings and Weak Willpower*, and a book about self-discipline for people who want to start exercising more – *How to Build Self-Discipline to Exercise: Practical Techniques and Strategies to Develop a Lifetime Habit of Exercise*.

Needless to say, I know a little and then some about self-discipline. As a lifelong businessperson, I realized I could help fellow entrepreneurs by writing a book dedicated to the unique challenges they face on a daily basis.

My business experience revolves around various online businesses. For a period of a few years I was a freelancer, mostly working in search engine optimization (SEO). I ran numerous small niche sites and monetized them with ad networks and affiliate programs. I had three e-commerce businesses selling physical products and digital products. I had a software-as-a-service (SaaS) business. I have an online self-publishing company, of which this book is the most recent fruit.

On the following pages, you'll discover how to weave self-discipline into your entrepreneurial fabric of life to help you achieve success in business. Drawing from my own experience of successful entrepreneurship and scientific research, I'll cover challenges of both new and seasoned entrepreneurs. We'll talk not only about how to develop but how to maintain self-discipline. You'll learn how to overcome common temptations of entrepreneurs and how to deal with some of the most common challenges that stop many of them in their tracks.

The primary aim of the book is to help you develop self-discipline and grit as an owner of a small business. I'm not here to tell you how to make a million dollars in five easy steps or build a seven-figure company with my foolproof blueprint. I'm not a business guru. In fact, I wouldn't even touch one with a ten-foot pole. My goal is to help you become a more self-disciplined entrepreneur, not tell you how to run a business.

Since this book can help all types of people who are self-employed, I'll interchangeably use words like "entrepreneur," "self-employed," and "businessperson" without differentiating between these terms.

At the end of each chapter I'll include the three most important actionable implications. Those are not there just for fun. Don't just read them—act on them. It's the only way this book will serve you.

I also conclude each chapter with a quick recap to help you revise the most important information. Repetition helps retain and review information.

Last but most definitely not least, a word of caution: the advice you're about to discover isn't set in stone. I don't believe in absolutes and I don't claim to have all of the answers. Consider the tips in this book to be ideas to test in your own life, but don't be afraid to try a different approach. Neither entrepreneurship nor self-discipline is an exact science. Different things can work for different people.

Now, let's talk about the first, most important part of building self-discipline as an entrepreneur (or for that matter, any other endeavor).

Chapter 1: Why Are You an Entrepreneur?

If you hope to build your self-discipline as an entrepreneur, you must have a strong motivation to *become* one and *stay* one. Entrepreneurship is not an easy path. If there's no strong motivator to keep you going when things are tough, you'll always struggle.

In this chapter we'll cover three types of motivation—extrinsic, intrinsic, and prosocial—and how they can help you maintain self-discipline as you to tie them all together to create a powerful fuel for your entrepreneurial endeavors.

Please don't think of your motivation as the magic pill. It's the foundation of it all, but it's not everything. Building a house starts with a foundation, but it doesn't end there. Having this in mind, let's move on to the three types of motivation and how they can help you stay disciplined as an entrepreneur.

Extrinsic Motivation

You might have started dreaming about entrepreneurship when you saw an exotic car on the street, a video of a luxurious mansion, or pictures of faraway tropical paradises.

Maybe you want to become an entrepreneur because of the status associated with being a CEO of your company, running a startup, or mingling with the powerful and wealthy.

Or maybe you have a business because you love seeing bigger and bigger numbers in your bank account or enjoy the feeling of a stack of banknotes in your wallet.

All these things are a manifestation of *extrinsic motivation*, which is being motivated by a reward, usually in a material sense.

Psychologists Richard M. Ryan and Edward L. Deci define extrinsic motivation as "a construct that pertains whenever an activity is done in order to attain some separable outcome."[i]

In layman's terms, extrinsic motivation is all about practicality and the end result itself. When you want to get a reward, you're motivated extrinsically. You're also motivated extrinsically when the desired outcome is to avoid some form of punishment. Grades in school are a form of extrinsic motivation serving both as a possible reward or punishment.

While extrinsic motivation is the most common type of motivation, it's also the weakest. It won't be sufficient to help you maintain self-discipline in the long term. It's weaker than the motivation coming from within (which we'll discuss later) because it's tied not to the self but to external rewards. If the reward is gone or the danger of punishment goes away, the motivation goes away with it.

For a new entrepreneur, extrinsic motivation can be about escaping the discomfort of having a day job. This type of motivation is often stronger than a positive motivation like the desire to own an expensive car or live in a big house because the need to escape pain can be stronger than the need to possess something.

Extrinsic goals that are about getting a reward—a new luxurious car, a villa, vacations, social status—

will motivate you, but once you get them (or stop desiring them before you achieve them), you'll have to come up with fresh motivators. It's not a good motivator if it's so transitory, don't you think?

For a period of time I wanted to buy a specific car. When I took it for a test drive, I didn't like driving it. As cool as it looked, suddenly I no longer cared about having one. If it had been my primary motivation to work on my business, I would be left without a good reason why.

And even if I did like it and had bought it, a few months later I wouldn't be motivated anymore because material things have a tendency to get old quickly. When we acquire what we want, we become satiated. Having bought the car, I would have to come up with a new toy I desired, thereby staying on the hamster wheel of purchasing new things for the temporary rush.

For this reason, I don't recommend making extrinsic motivators your primary reasons to start or grow your business. By all means, make a list of all the nice things you'd like to have, but be aware they're not the strongest motivators you can have.

I like to use extrinsic motivation in the form of punishment, also known as *push motivation*. I know an entrepreneur who writes his friends checks for $100, telling them to cash them if he doesn't finish a specific business task he's been procrastinating on recently.

As much as you'd like to love all business tasks, there will always be unpleasant things to do. Motivating yourself to do them to escape punishment can work well, as long as the punishment is worse than performing the task you need to do.

Having a list of all the things you want to buy, places you want to visit, or the status you'll enjoy can be helpful, but it will never match the power of...

Intrinsic Motivation

Maybe you started a business because you felt that being an employee was clashing with your sense of autonomy or killing you from the inside.

Perhaps you're an entrepreneur or want to become one because you crave challenges and personal growth, and want full control over your life.

Maybe you have a business because you want to realize your potential and you know it's impossible to do so working for somebody else.

Or perhaps you simply love being an entrepreneur and it's a lifetime addiction for you.

This is *intrinsic motivation*. It's stronger than extrinsic motivation because it comes from within you and is not dependent on an external reward or punishment.

Psychologists Richard M. Ryan and Edward L. Deci define intrinsic motivation as "the doing of an activity for its inherent satisfactions rather than for some separable consequence. When intrinsically motivated a person is moved to act for the fun or challenge entailed rather than because of external prods, pressures, or rewards."[ii]

Intrinsic motivation deals with what you feel inside. It can be a feeling of fun, having a challenge, or the need for independence and control. If you want to become a self-disciplined entrepreneur, the strongest intrinsic motivator you'll ever find is independence.

Nothing tastes better than the ability to do what you want, when you want, where you want, and with whom you want. No car, villa, designer clothes, or jewelry will sustain your self-discipline more than the addictive feeling of being the master of your life.

Now, mind you, that's obviously not a conclusion of a scientific study. However, if you look at successful entrepreneurs, you'll find a common link between virtually all of them. They are driven by the desire to have the freedom to do what they want, not the need to show off with a new expensive car or a flashy villa.

A good example is British billionaire Richard Branson, who said, "My golden rule for business and life is: We should all enjoy what we do and do what we enjoy."[iii]

Canadian-American billionaire Elon Musk also often refers to his intrinsic motivation. He is motivated by challenges. In his words: "I think life on

Earth must be about more than just solving problems… It's got to be something inspiring even if it is vicarious."

He also believes in enjoyment: "People work better when they know what the goal is and why. It is important that people look forward to coming to work in the morning and enjoy working."[iv]

Constant improvement is yet another type of intrinsic motivation that can keep you going for a lifetime. As Sergey Brin, co-founder of Google said, improvement has no bounds: "It's clear there is a lot of room for improvement, there's no inherent ceiling we're hitting up on."[v]

A word of caution regarding extrinsic and intrinsic motivation:

Because of the overjustification effect, extrinsic motivators like money or prizes can *decrease* a person's intrinsic motivation to perform a task.[vi] The activity ceases to be about enjoyment, personal challenge, or self-growth and becomes purely about what tangible things you can get out of it.

For instance, in sports, the performance of many professional athletes declines after signing a multimillion-dollar contract. Their "hunger" disappears overnight. For this reason, it's of vital importance to prioritize intrinsic motivation over extrinsic motivation and be careful not to give too much of a weight to external rewards.

When you compare intrinsic motivation, which is an endless source of inspiration, to extrinsic motivation, which is fleeting, it's clear that intrinsic motivation will serve you longer and better.

However, there's yet another way to guarantee you'll keep going despite setbacks and stay persistent no matter the obstacles. It's...

Prosocial Motivation

Psychologists might argue that the only two "legitimate" types of motivation are extrinsic and intrinsic motivation. However, there's a third type of motivation that is neither extrinsic nor intrinsic.

If you want to grow your business because you want to support your family, you're motivated socially, for the benefit of your loved ones.

If you run what entrepreneur Yanik Silver calls an "evolved enterprise" (a company that ties its existence to supporting a specific charitable goal),[vii] you might be motivated by the need to help the needy, environment, or otherwise change the world for the better.

Adam Grant, professor and bestselling author of *Give and Take: A Revolutionary Approach to Success,* suggests in a paper on intrinsic motivation and prosocial behaviors that the desire to help others makes us go the extra mile.[viii]

It's more effective as a motivator than intrinsic motivation alone, but for the best results you should combine both. In the author's words, "employees display higher levels of persistence, performance, and productivity when they experience prosocial and intrinsic motivations in tandem."

When starting your business or growing it, find a prosocial reason to do so. It might be to benefit a specific cause or a group of people.

Think about tying your company's performance with the causes you'd like to support. For instance,

Californian-based online marketplace Sevenly donates 7% of its revenue to charitable causes. In five years it raised over $4 million dollars to support and spread awareness about the causes it supports.[ix]

At one point, adding more numbers to your bank account won't improve your happiness. Consequently, it will no longer be as motivating as before. A person who goes from making $20,000 a year to $60,000 will most likely get noticeably happier. A person who makes $5 million a year won't feel any different when they start making six, seven, or eight million.

According to Princeton researchers Angus Deaton and Daniel Kahneman, the threshold is a yearly income of around $75,000. After crossing this number, making more money can improve your perception of your life, but it isn't going to do much to improve your emotional well-being.[x] Obviously this number is for the United States and can be lower or higher depending on where you live; it's approximately 150% of the national median salary.

After you cross $75,000 a year, money might cease to be a strong motivator. It doesn't apply to prosocial motivation, though. You can always dedicate more resources to support your favorite charitable causes. It always has a direct impact, and it never gets old and pointless as simply spending more money on new toys.

If you don't believe in charity, you don't have to support any organizations. It doesn't have to be about money. Your prosocial motivation might be dedicated solely to just one person who becomes your "who" instead of "why"—the person who will benefit from your success. In most cases, it will be your loved ones: your children, spouse, siblings, or parents.

For instance, my strongest prosocial motivation to succeed in business was to make enough money to help my parents realize their lifetime dream of moving to the countryside.

My extrinsic motivators were never even ten percent as motivating as this goal. Even my powerful intrinsic motivators were still second to helping my parents, who have spent so many years taking care of me to ensure I would get everything I needed to succeed in life.

For a parent, a primary prosocial motivator can be the need to spend as much time as they want with their child. A successful business can provide income, but it can also provide something more valuable—ample free time.

Whatever or whoever you want to support, I can't overemphasize the power of prosocial motivation. Think beyond yourself.

Three Key Actionable Implications

Now that you know three types of motivation, you might wonder how to apply them in your life. The three most important actionable implications are:

1. Switch "Ferrari" for "Freedom"

Many self-help gurus claim that the most powerful motivator you can have is to create a vision board and look at it every single day to remind yourself why you're chasing your goals. I won't say this strategy doesn't work; it does, though it's not half as powerful as the less tangible reasons for entrepreneurial success such as the freedom and independence it will give you.

A car can give only fleeting happiness. Freedom—once attained—will deliver permanent enjoyment and inspiration. Unlike a new car, it never gets old and, if anything, only gets better with time.

By all means, motivate yourself with rewards if you want to, but make them supplemental to your primary intrinsic and prosocial motivators. Come up with these motivators now.

2. Use Push Motivation to Handle Procrastination

Push motivation relies on external factors that force you to complete a specific task to avoid a certain consequence. It doesn't work well to keep your motivation in the long term (just ask any student anywhere in the world), but it can be useful to create a bout of motivation to overcome the reluctance to start working on a task you've been procrastinating on for a long time.

Setting financial stakes works particularly well since they're easy to set up and painful if you fail to act on them. Another type of push motivation can be an accountability group or a coach who will require weekly reports from you and give you a hard time if you fail to accomplish what you've promised to do.

Find a way to hold yourself accountable or set stakes to push yourself to do hard tasks you always put off.

3. Go Beyond Yourself

Make your goals not only about yourself. Include others, whether they're your loved ones, strangers in need, animals, environment, science, or arts. Whatever cause you believe in, a prosocial motivation will strengthen your resolve.

Think of it this way: anyone would jump into a dangerous river to save their drowning child, while few people would jump into the same roaring river to retrieve a dropped $100 dollar bill.

There isn't and never will be a more powerful motivator than extending your goal beyond yourself. When you combine it with a strong set of intrinsic motivators and support it every now and then with extrinsic punishments, you'll have a solid base upon which you can build long-term self-discipline.

If you already have a list of motivators, ask yourself how you can extend them to others. Keep it in mind whenever you feel discouraged or tempted to give up.

WHY ARE YOU AN ENTREPRENEUR: QUICK RECAP

1. To strengthen your resolve to succeed, the first step is to discover your motivations. If you know one or more powerful reasons why you want to make your business succeed, you'll be less likely to give up or slow down when facing obstacles.

2. Extrinsic motivation deals with things in the external world—cars, houses, the size of your bank account, status, envy, and other similar kinds of rewards. It's also about escaping punishment. This type of motivation is helpful, but not half as powerful as intrinsic and prosocial motivation.

3. Intrinsic motivation comes from within. It's about the fun of doing something, the challenge of it, growth, independence, freedom, or having control over your life.

If as your guiding star you use independence—unlike, for example, buying an expensive car that will become boring a few months after the purchase—it will become a permanent and renewable source of inspiration to keep you working and growing as an entrepreneur.

4. Prosocial motivation is the strongest motivator. If you're building a business not only to benefit yourself, but also others, you'll be more persistent, productive, and effective. Combining a socially motivated reason with your intrinsic motivation will result in a strong foundation for self-discipline.

Chapter 2: Creating a Lifestyle Centered Around Self-Discipline

It can be easier to maintain self-discipline as an entrepreneur if you structure your life in a way conducive to it. In this chapter we'll talk about different ways in which you can change your mindset and default behaviors to thrive as an entrepreneur, even when you find yourself in less than ideal circumstances.

Many of these changes are simple, but not necessarily easy. However, making an effort will be well worth the benefits: gaining more self-discipline, becoming more persistent, and living a happier life.

Get the Right Input

If you don't have many friends who are entrepreneurs, you may find yourself feeling lonely or misunderstood. A lack of or inadequate support makes it harder to maintain self-discipline and stay persistent. For this reason, it's crucial to pay attention to your social environment.

People closest to you, like your friends and family, have the biggest impact on you. Entrepreneur and motivational speaker Jim Rohn once said, "You're the average of the five people you spend most of your time with."

There's no scientific research proving it's exactly five people, but there's research suggesting that we can indeed adapt new behaviors purely through observation. It's called *social learning theory* and posits that we learn from our immediate surroundings.

The creator of the theory, Albert Bandura, proposes that people can learn by observing a behavior of another person in three ways:[xi]

- Live model – In which we directly see another person demonstrating a certain behavior,

- Verbal instruction – In which we're instructed by another person how to engage in a certain behavior,

- Symbolic – In which we model behaviors of real or fictional characters from movies, television, Internet, literature, and radio.

What's important to note is that we can acquire undesirable behaviors unconsciously. For instance, research shows that children and young adults playing violent video games exhibit more aggressive behavior.[xii] Watching violent television is also correlated with aggressive behavior.[xiii] When you confront them about that, though, few (if any) would agree that they have unconsciously learned to be more aggressive.

Now, what does all of this have in common with you, an entrepreneur who wants to become more self-disciplined?

It shows that your immediate surroundings—including your friends, family, and the media content you consume on a daily basis—can affect how disciplined you are, and it can happen without your conscious participation.

Consequently, make sure to get input that promotes successful behaviors and habits, not destructive ones. If you hang out with lazy people whose primary goal in life is to get wasted on the weekends, don't expect to achieve much success in business. On the other hand, if you spend a great deal of time with successful entrepreneurs, you'll most likely become one soon.

In addition to that, social psychologist Roy F. Baumeister suggests that positive emotions can potentially replenish willpower.[xiv] Unambitious, whiny friends aren't likely to arouse many positive emotions in you, while growth-oriented people definitely do. All in all, there's a lot to gain by paying attention to your social surroundings, isn't there?

The three most important steps to turn your social environment into a more empowering one are:

1. Filter Your Friends

Divide your friends into two groups: people who help you grow, and people who drag you down. Then reduce or stop spending time with the second group.

Okay, I admit that it sounds a little cruel, but listen to a little story.

I have a childhood friend who comes from a well-educated middle class family. He used to be a nice kid who stayed away from problems. When I moved to a foreign country for a few months, we lost contact. During this time he made new friends—unambitious, lazy people you wouldn't like your child to hang out with.

Soon, he started smoking, drinking more alcohol than before, and engaging in other irresponsible behaviors. I had a hard time accepting his new "self." I couldn't help him change his ways because of the enormous impact his other friends had on him.

It was only when he cut ties with those destructive friends he stopped engaging in negative behaviors. Only then we could, to an extent, resurrect our friendship, and he could start rebuilding his life. I'm sure that if it hadn't been for his decision to stop associating with these individuals he would still be there, sitting on a bench smoking illegal substances, if not dealing drugs.

Does it still sound cruel to filter your friends? Obviously most of us don't hang around drug dealers or lazy potheads. However, remember that all kinds of behaviors in our immediate surroundings can affect us. If your closest friends don't think about the future, always seek immediate comfort and security, and never act on their goals (if they even have them), what will you learn from them?

Your social circle doesn't have to consist of entrepreneurs only. It's not as much about entrepreneurship as it's about being with people who make you better. I have a friend who's a model employee, while in contrast I'm an unemployable entrepreneur. However, he wants to grow as a person, and that's something positive you want to have in your life.

Make sure that your social circle contributes to your growth, and regularly pull out weeds. There's no point in spending time with people who don't want you to become better.

Please keep in mind, though, that I don't condone being a fair-weather friend or calculating in cold blood who should be allowed to be in your life. It's not about leaving friends who have problems because their problems might affect you or avoiding people who are less successful than you. It's about filtering out people who suck the energy out of you, envy your success, and sabotage your efforts to better yourself.

2. Avoid Mainstream Media

For the sake of maintaining my sanity and positive outlook on the world, I've been on a low information diet for years. The general premise is to avoid all kinds of unproductive news, particularly bad news from mainstream media.[xv] I don't remember the last time I've accessed a news site or bought a newspaper to read what's happening in the world. And I feel great about it.

Media thrives on negativity, fear, violence, and hate. Don't believe me? Open any newspaper or visit a news site and count positive and negative headlines. Good luck finding more than a handful of positive news items among a sea of terrorist attacks, accidents, natural disasters, political feuds, financial crises, and every other flavor of negativity there is.

Consuming bad news on a daily basis is not only a waste of time but also poses a threat to your general well-being. Research shows that watching negative news makes you worry more, and this in turn exacerbates your own personal worries and anxieties.[xvi]

How do you expect to be persistent and self-disciplined with such a negative attitude?

Moreover, media dramatically inflates the perception of risk of a regular person. When you read about tragic events every day, it's easy to develop a belief that the world is a dangerous place, which can make you risk-averse. Since uncertainty and risk-taking are necessities for every entrepreneur, consuming bad news directly affects the results you get as a businessperson.

Stop consuming low-calorie information, stay away from news, gossip, and fearmongering. If something important happens in the world, you'll hear about it anyway from your friends or family. As for the rest—why fill your life with so much negativity?

3. Feed Your Mind with Positivity

Thanks to the Internet, it's equally easy to find both positive and negative content. Most people stick to the latter, but by now you know the more intelligent choice is to ignore it and focus on the former.

Instead of spending time on news or gossip sites, find sites that promote positivity, happiness, and personal growth. Join forums for people who want to improve themselves or their businesses. Read self-help blogs. Watch motivational videos.

The point isn't necessarily to pump yourself up. The goal is to feed your mind with positive input on a daily basis to encourage the development of productive beliefs and habits.

Surround yourself with positivity in your offline world as well. Spend more time with happy people who make you smile. Visit venues where positive people hang out. Read empowering books that promote hope, inspiration, and optimism.

You don't have to see everything through rose-colored glasses or deny that bad things happen. The idea is to cleanse yourself of all the negative input and replace it with things more conducive to growth.

The more positive models you have—people, books, websites, movies, music—the more positive you'll become. This will translate into more persistence, self-discipline, and willpower, no matter the circumstances in your life.

Avoid These Five Negative Behaviors at All Costs

Regularly repeated negative behaviors can train you to act in a way that's not conducive to your entrepreneurial success. Here are five destructive actions to immediately eliminate from your life:

1. Complaining

Complaining is the epitome of wasting time. Instead of working on the solution to a problem, you point out how it's wrong, unfair, or otherwise bad for you.

Did you know that complaining can cause extensive damage to your mind and body? In an interview with *Stanford News*, neuroscientist Robert

Sapolsky points out that experiencing non-life-threatening stressors on a daily basis triggers the unnecessary release of adrenalin and other stress hormones, which, over time, contribute to many leading causes of death in the Western world.

In his words: "If you plan to get stressed like a normal mammal, you had better turn on the stress response or else you're dead. But if you get chronically, psychosocially stressed, like a Westernized human, then you are more at risk for heart disease and some of the other leading causes of death in Westernized life."[xvii]

Sapolsky's research suggests that stress hormones cause atrophy of the hippocampus, the part of the brain associated primarily with long-term memory. How would you feel about complaining when you imagine it's literally shrinking a part of your brain?

Motivational speaker Les Brown once posted these words on his Facebook page:

"Refuse to complain. Complaining is just a way of not taking responsibility, justifying doing nothing, and programming yourself to fail. Complaining creates the illusion that you have done something. Instead, pour your energy into improving your situation. When you find ways to be productive and maintain a sense of optimism, you demonstrate that you are in control of your own life.

"Complainers focus on what has happened, and give up their power. Winners focus on making things happen, and using their power to find solutions to their challenges. You were born to create something magnificent with your life! Solution-based thinking gives you that power."[xviii]

As an entrepreneur, your job is to solve problems. Complaining solves absolutely nothing. Replace negativity with a list of possible solutions and act on them. Develop a habit of taking the lead instead of victimizing yourself.

Speaking of which, the second negative habit is…

2. Resignation

The entrepreneurial life is a constant rollercoaster for any new entrepreneur. It's common to feel resigned when you're on a long way down after a previous high.

However, the longer you brood over your flops and setbacks, the deeper you'll go into a depressive state of mind that may cause you to give up rather than work on your goals.

I've had more than my fair share of failures as an entrepreneur. I've been in debt. My businesses have failed overnight. I've invested thousands of dollars and countless hours into projects that were a complete disaster.

Each time I got dealt a blow, I felt reluctant to try again. However, by not allowing myself to spend more a day or two in such a stupor I've always managed to get back up, dust myself off, and try again. Without exception, what helped me was turning myself to hope and inspiration and away from the doom and gloom of resigning myself to fate.

Whenever you feel down, by all means let yourself feel bad for a while if that's what you need, but then—as hard as it is—start devising another plan. Make a rough outline of action steps you'll take when you're ready for a next ride.

3. Jealousy

When you're envious of the success of others, it's easy to think, "oh, he got it easy," or come up with other ways of discrediting somebody's success or finding excuses other than simple persistence and dedication.

If you consider successful individuals as people who "got lucky," what kind of a message does your subconscious get? How persistent will you be if deep down you think that entrepreneurial success is all about luck, privileges, or being immoral?

Your subconscious will work against you if deep down you're jealous and despise successful people.

Replace envy with appreciation. Each time you hear about a successful person, see it as proof that you can achieve success, too. Better yet, start hanging out with successful people and learn from them.

4. Scarcity Mentality

Scarcity mentality is thinking that success is a zero-sum game. If there's a cake on the table and you grab a big slice of it, there'll be less of the cake for everyone else.

It might apply to cakes, but it doesn't apply to success.

Sharing your knowledge with others doesn't make you less intelligent. Loving one of your children doesn't mean there's less love to go around for everybody else. And if you become a successful entrepreneur, it doesn't mean that somebody else had to go bankrupt.

Abundance mentality is the opposite of scarcity mentality. It's about the belief there's always more to go around, that you can always create more, and that you can achieve more with the help of others instead of competing against them for supposedly scarce resources.

Wharton's youngest tenured professor, Adam Grant, writes in his bestselling book *Give and Take: Why Helping Others Drives Our Success*, "This is what I find most magnetic about successful givers: they get to the top without cutting others down, finding ways of expanding the pie that benefit themselves and the people around them. Whereas success is zero-sum in a group of takers, in groups of givers, it may be true that the whole is greater than the sum of the parts."[xix]

You too can enjoy this synergic effect if you focus on giving and sharing resources instead of hoarding everything for yourself.

In his bestselling book *Make It Big: 49 Secrets for Building a Life of Extreme Success,* successful real estate investor Frank McKinney writes, "When you give more than you expect to receive, you are coming from a place of strength within yourself. You stop being a bookkeeper always trying to keep score, and instead become a philanthropist, knowing there is enough for you to be generous. And ultimately, with this attitude you do receive just as much."[xx]

As counterintuitive as it sounds, to get more, give more. Turn from a go-getter into a go-giver and you'll go a long way. [xxi]

5. Giving Up Early and Often

You reinforce what you repeat on a regular basis. If you have a habit of giving up early, you'll have a hard time persevering.

If you quickly lose enthusiasm when learning a new skill, why would it be different when starting a business or testing new business ideas?

If you throw up your hands the moment you face an obstacle—say, you don't know how to do something—you train yourself to become helpless.

According to a thesis by Diana Lynn Bartolotta at the Carnegie Mellon University, optimists work longer at tasks they perceive to be important.[xxii] What's interesting is that pessimists persist longer when confronted with unimportant tasks while optimists tend to give up more quickly when they perceive a task to be trivial.

Bartolotta concludes the research paper by saying, "a pessimist is more likely to waste his time and energy over trivial tasks, while an optimist conserves his time and energy for the more important tasks. Consequently, optimists will fare better on more important tasks."

Develop a more persistence-friendly attitude by developing the belief that you can push through obstacles and doing so whenever you find yourself in a difficult situation.

Engage in activities that require patience, learn complex skills, or put yourself in situations that require problem-solving skills. The more often you stay with the problem longer and persevere, the easier it will be to keep going with your other goals, too.

Three Key Actionable Implications

To help you implement the advice from this chapter, here are the three key actionable implications:

1. Restructure Your Surroundings

Think about who and what contributes positively to your surroundings and who or what makes it harder to maintain self-discipline or be an optimist.

I suggest rating the most important factors using a scale of 1 to 10 (1 being the least negative and 10 having the most poisonous impact) and then getting rid of the negative influences one by one, starting from the ones with the highest score.

It might be a specific person; a habit that always makes your days worse, like complaining; or perhaps a part of your everyday routine like getting up too late and then not having time and energy to work on your goals after taking care of other pressing obligations.

2. Become Proactive

Complaining and resignation are two common destructive behaviors that lead to self-victimization.

If you wait for things to happen instead of making them happen yourself, it's highly unlikely you'll ever become a successful entrepreneur.

Train yourself to resist the temptation to throw up your hands in resignation. Instead, take action to solve the problem and appreciate it as a challenge to strengthen your resolve.

As Arnold Schwarzenegger said in an interview for the *Boston Globe*, "Strength does not come from winning. Your struggles develop your strengths. When you go through hardships and decide not to surrender, that is strength."[xxiii]

Proactivity is also about preparing for possible future problems. If you were to go on a diet, wouldn't getting rid of all unhealthy foods in your home make more sense than tapping into your willpower each time you went to the kitchen?

Even if you were the most self-disciplined entrepreneur in the world, wouldn't you rather avoid temptations by being proactive than waiting for things to happen?

3. Give More

One of the worst negative behaviors you can engage in is thinking that resources are scarce and that you should keep everything to yourself. When you're afraid of sharing your knowledge, time, and money with others, you build a cage that might be successful at turning you into a miser, but won't help you achieve long-term success.

Starting today, make an effort to give more. If you're a writer, share some of your writings for free. If you sell physical products, throw in a gift. Share your experience with others with no strings attached.

You'll eradicate scarcity mentality from your life when you continuously and generously share what you have with others and always think in terms of expanding the pie for everyone.

CREATING A LIFESTYLE CENTERED AROUND SELF-DISCIPLINE: QUICK RECAP

1. People around you can influence you in a positive or a negative way. You can unconsciously adopt the negative behaviors and beliefs of people around you. For this reason, it's important to be mindful of whom you let inside your social circle, as some people can drag you down and sabotage your efforts to better yourself.

2. If you want to turn your surroundings into more empowering ones, filter your friends, avoid mainstream media, and feed your mind with positivity.

Filtering your friends is about consciously choosing with whom you hang out. Remember that other people can promote behaviors that aren't conducive to your personal success or simply drain your energy for the fun of it.

It's important to avoid mainstream media because it features almost exclusively negative news designed to make you feel afraid, threatened, and uneasy. It also inflates your perception of risk. A constant influx of negative thoughts isn't beneficial to your success, or to anything, for that matter. Get rid of this self-imposed torture.

Feeding your mind with positivity is about consuming inspirational, empowering content and hanging out with individuals who share your positivity. It can be inspirational videos. Happy people. Forums with users who want to improve themselves. You choose what to put in your mind; why not ensure it's beneficial input that will make you a happier and more successful person?

3. Five behaviors that can dramatically weaken your resolve as an entrepreneur are complaining, resignation, jealousy, scarcity mentality, and giving up early and often.

Complaining develops a habit of grumbling about problems instead of coming up with solutions. It also leads to self-victimization, which kills persistence.

Resignation leaves you unable to take action. The longer you let yourself feel fatalistic, the more difficult it will be to get up and try again. Let yourself feel bad for a while if you need it, but don't wait too long to devise a new plan.

Attributing the success of other people to things you can't control, like privileges or good luck, is like telling yourself that persistence doesn't work. Don't expect to achieve success if you criticize successful people instead of being appreciative of the example they set for others.

Scarcity mentality is thinking that everything in this world is scarce, and thus you should hoard everything for yourself. Such mentality will sabotage your goals because you'll live in constant fear of losing your precious limited resources, and it will alienate you from others because you'll be afraid to share your knowledge and collaborate.

Giving up early—in all kinds of contexts, not just business—develops a destructive habit that ensures you'll never score any huge wins. Everything worthwhile takes time to achieve, so it's key to train yourself to keep going longer than everyone else.

Chapter 3: How to Keep Balance and Stay Sane

Entrepreneurship isn't just a career choice. For most, entrepreneurship is a lifestyle, attitude, and a state of mind all at once.

If you work for somebody else, you don't have to worry about the business 24/7. You get paid for your contribution to the company and nothing more, so it's easier to mark the line between your personal and professional life.

If you own a business, you can't switch your mind off and forget about it. It's like your baby. You think about it every single day, even when you're on vacation. This can both serve you and work to your detriment.

In this chapter we'll explore how to keep balance and maintain sanity as you work on your business.

Your Body Is Your CEO

Entrepreneurs like to consider themselves heroes who can work 24/7 without rest. Many are tempted to believe their bodies are infallible machines able to run exclusively on coffee and snacks. They also delude themselves thinking they can push their personal lives to the side and fix everything later, after they achieve business success.

Hate to break it to you, but living in such a way will inevitably destroy your health, relationships, and general well-being.

When it comes to health, your body is your CEO, and it *will* fire you if you keep disrespecting it. Taking care of your health means having a healthy diet, exercising, getting enough sleep, and avoiding unhealthy habits. It's paramount to your success as an entrepreneur.

A healthy diet is necessary to get all of the nutrients your body needs. Unprocessed food is the best choice here, both for health and satiety. If you put low-quality food in your body, you'll get low-quality performance.

As for exercise, in her book *The Willpower Instinct: How Self-Control Works, Why It Matters, and What You Can Do to Get More of It,* psychologist and bestselling author Kelly McGonigal states, "exercise turns out to be the closest thing to a wonder drug that self-control scientists have discovered. For starters, the willpower benefits of exercise are immediate. Fifteen minutes on a treadmill reduces cravings, as seen when researchers try to tempt dieters with chocolate and smokers with cigarettes."[xxiv]

As for sleep, research by Roy F. Baumeister suggests that rest can replenish your willpower.[xxv] If this fact alone doesn't persuade you, consider that sleep deprivation produces cognitive and motor impairments equivalent to a legally intoxicating blood-alcohol level.[xxvi] I don't think I need to tell you about other benefits of getting enough sleep, do I?

You can learn much more about living a healthy lifestyle in my books *Self-Disciplined Dieter* and *How to Build Self-Discipline to Exercise*.

What's important to emphasize in relation to self-discipline is that if you neglect your health, sooner or later you'll have to pay the dues. The longer you neglect proper care of your health, the less effective you'll become. This will then translate into decreased self-discipline.

Your health should never take a backseat. You can always resume your entrepreneurial ventures, but you can't always regain your health.

Four Reasons and Solutions to Work-Life Imbalance

True entrepreneurial success isn't only about your profits, sales, revenue, and valuations – it's also about finding proper balance to enjoy *both* your business and your personal life. Otherwise, what's the point? Entrepreneurial success means nothing if you've failed at relationships.

In his article on work-life balance for *Forbes*, entrepreneur Michael Simmons shares four reasons why, according to entrepreneur coach David Kashen, work-life balance is so hard for entrepreneurs.[xxvii] Let's deconstruct and remedy each of these challenges one by one:

1. Intermingling of Personal Identity and Business Well-Being

When you treat your business as your baby, it's easy for the line between personal and business life to blur. Emotional attachment to your company can then determine your well-being. If business is good, you feel good. If business is bad, so do you.

As a logical-thinking human being, you don't want to feel bad. Consequently, you spend more and more time working so you can constantly monitor your business and attend to its needs. Soon, there's no balance whatsoever in your life because everything revolves around your business.

How do you solve this problem?

If the primary reason is associating your self-worth with your business performance, the solution is to find more roles that will define you as a person and draw self-worth out of these roles, too. When you're not only an entrepreneur, but also a parent, a spouse, a tennis player, or an active participant in your local community, your self-worth is less prone to break when you encounter problems in one area of your life.

It may seem counterintuitive, but you can become a much better entrepreneur if you don't think about business all the time. Other roles in your life can help you step away and see the forest for the trees.

Lastly, consider delegation as an additional way to break the bond between your self-esteem and your business. Ceding some responsibilities to other people can help you stop thinking of your business in terms of something only *you* can take care of and grow.

2. Fear of Failure

For many entrepreneurs, their company is everything they have. They've put all of their resources in it: life savings, time, energy, and reputation. As a result, many of them struggle to balance between their personal and professional lives.

How can you avoid this common pitfall?

The first step is to change your relationship with failure. Fear is a useful emotion when you face a predator in the bushes, but it's not a productive state of mind for an entrepreneur.

Fear of failure is usually the strongest for a person who hasn't experienced a lot of failures in life.

Why not undergo a "failure therapy" by purposefully trying difficult things with a high probability of failure? We fear things because they're unknown. If you experience something on a daily basis—like failure, in this case—it ceases to be scary.

I failed countless times as an entrepreneur. As bad as all of these failures were, they also taught me to feel comfortable with them.

Face your fear and invite failure in your life. You don't necessarily have to purposefully fail in your business. To become accustomed to obstacles, setbacks, and slip-ups, invite challenges in your personal life, like learning a new and difficult skill.

The second step to deal with a fear of failure—when it's motivated by a fear of losing money—is to get your financial life in order. Your fear of failure will diminish if you create a fund that will cover your living expenses for six months in case of an emergency. This will also allow you to feel more comfortable taking a break, going on vacation, or spending time enjoying other aspects of your life than business.

3. Love of Work

Listen, I get it. You're extremely passionate about your business and you think about it all the time. I'm wired the same way. You can't turn off my entrepreneurial mind. It's all fine unless business is the sole passion in your life and becomes your only escape from problems.

If the imbalance in your life is primarily motivated by your passion for the business and it starts to strain your relationships, it's time for a change.

What helped me personally was finding other passions beyond work. I then infected others with some of them. For instance, I regularly go rock climbing with a friend. I also have a love of languages and travel, so planning future trips is another passionate activity that takes away my attention from business.

Find non-business passions in your life, and if you get addicted to them, they'll help you achieve more balance in life. As a side benefit, you'll be more energized and have fresh perspectives for how to grow your business.

4. A Reward for Getting More Work Done

As an entrepreneur, you can always work more and always achieve more. There's no ceiling to how much you can achieve, and it feels great to constantly achieve more. It's not surprising that many entrepreneurs work as much as they can and still feel they should work more.

Unfortunately, this addiction to achievement comes with negative side effects. You start neglecting your health, family, friends, and self-care. At one point, a simple desire to work more turns into workaholism, an addiction to work for the sake of working.

The solution to this problem is similar to the solution regarding the love of work. Find something that will challenge you and make you feel productive. It doesn't have to generate tangible results directly; as long as it gives you a similar feeling of achievement you get thanks to your business, it will do. You get bonus points for doing this activity with others.

For instance, I love learning languages and consider it an extremely productive way of spending time. It reminds me there's more to achieve in life than just in my business, and that helps me balance better between my personal and entrepreneurial life. I also practice various sports including tennis and cycling, and invite my friends to enjoy them with me.

To further regain balance, engage in these purposeful and productive pastimes with other people in your life. Find personal satisfaction in spending quality time with your loved ones *and* doing something that develops you as a person. Here are some ideas:

- Join a local football team with your friends.

- Get yourself and your family interested in exploring the wilderness and organize regular trips.

- Build something with your own hands: a kitchen table, a toy, a home decoration. Invite your friends, kids, spouse, or other family members to participate.

- Cook something. Cooking and eating are some of the most pleasant social activities that will put a smile on your face and make you feel a sense of accomplishment.

- Practice various arts: painting, music-making, writing, sculpting. Engage your entire family or share the fruits of your work with them.

- Get into gardening. It will help you unwind. You can also turn it into a social activity with your spouse, kids, or friends who don't mind getting their hands dirty.

The bottom line is to have a life beyond your business. Finding excitement in non-business contexts will make it easier to maintain balance between your personal and professional life.

In addition to these four reasons, your life might be out of balance because you don't know how to structure it in another way. If you need help with that, I wrote a book dedicated entirely to this topic titled *How to Have More Time*. It includes tips that will help you reduce time spent working, change your lifestyle to make more space for time, and turn from a money-rich, time-poor person into a money-rich and time-rich individual.

Three Key Actionable Implications

Below are three key actionable implications to help you maintain proper balance in life and stay sane.

1. Take Care of Your Health

Entrepreneurial ventures are addictive and provide a lot of enjoyment. However, if you neglect your health, one day you might find yourself no longer able to work. Basic prevention is all it takes to minimize the risk of developing many serious illnesses.

Analyze your health and fitness levels. Do you have a healthy diet? Do you get enough exercise and sleep? Do you treat your body as your boss that needs to be respected or as a slave you regularly run into the ground?

If you're overweight, change your eating habits and exercise more. Get more sleep if you tend to pull all-nighters and frequently find yourself falling asleep in the middle of the day.

Ideally, find a way to derive passion and enjoyment out of your efforts to improve your health and fitness. If you need help, my books *Self-Disciplined Dieter: How to Lose Weight and Become Healthy Despite Cravings and Weak Willpower* and *How to Build Self-Discipline to Exercise: Practical Techniques and Strategies to Develop a Lifetime Habit of Exercise* will help you.

2. Set Non-Business Challenges

If the only accomplishments in your life come from business, it's no wonder you tend to prioritize it over your personal life. After all, humans want to feel good, and if it's primarily business achievement that fuels you, where else would you seek personal satisfaction?

Come up with a new hobby, a skill you want to master, or an improvement you'd like to make in your personal life. This will help you satisfy your hunger for accomplishment and stop measuring your self-worth by your business performance alone. Let yourself win and lose in your personal life, which will bring more excitement to your life from other sources than just your business.

I strongly suggest practicing at least one difficult sport that will take your mind off business, help you unwind, and present a challenge so you don't have to escape to work as a form of self-therapy.

3. Have a Life

I get it, you adore your business. You love entrepreneurship. It's your passion. However, as preposterous of an idea as it sounds, you should still have a life outside of it. Businesspeople who rarely, if ever, think about other things than business tend to overwork themselves to death, neglect their personal lives, and end up unhappy.

Don't forget that your life consists of more than just being productive. Take care of your health and fitness, spend quality time with your family and friends, and try to grow yourself as a person beyond business context. All these things, when combined, will help you achieve your results much more quickly, and in a more pleasant way, than becoming a lonely workaholic.

Today, right now, come up with a plan to have a more satisfying personal life. If you wake up each day passionate only about your business, but not about your personal life, it's high time to change it and start looking forward to being a regular, non-work-addicted human being as well.

HOW TO KEEP BALANCE AND STAY SANE: QUICK RECAP

1. Your body is your CEO. Don't neglect your health, thinking that you'll have time for it later when you achieve success. Your overall sense of well-being greatly contributes to your self-discipline and persistence. How do you see yourself reaching big goals if you're sick and exhausted all the time?

2. There are four primary reasons why you can't achieve proper work-life balance: intermingling of personal identity and business well-being, fear of failure, love of work, and the feeling of a reward for getting more work done.

Intermingling of personal identity and business well-being means that you let your business define your self-worth. Such a close link with your business causes you to spend more and more time with it until there's nothing else going in your life but work.

Handle this problem by finding more roles in your life that can define your self-worth (like being a good parent). Additionally, realize that you can achieve more success by letting yourself step away from the business and see it from another perspective. Last but not least, delegate parts of your business so it doesn't feel like your sole responsibility.

Fear of failure makes entrepreneurs work crazy hours and sacrifice their personal lives. A typical entrepreneur is heavily invested in their business, both financially and emotionally.

Learning how to feel comfortable with discomfort by inviting failure in your life will help you reduce the worries about your business failing. Insure yourself by building an emergency financial fund. Fear of failure won't be that crippling and dominant in your life if you know that even in the worst case you'll be able to support yourself financially for a few months.

Love of work sounds like a good thing, but entrepreneurs often take it to the extreme and let business become the only source of challenges and self-fulfillment. Find hobbies outside business that will challenge you to break the spell of business being the only source of passion in life.

A reward you get for more work done feels good. As an entrepreneur, you can always get more of this reward as there's always more that you can do. Unfortunately, this also means that it's easy to go overboard with it and neglect everything else.

This problem ties with love of work. If business is the only addictive thing in your life, it's obvious that you'll prioritize it over everything else. As hard as it might be, come up with non-business activities— ideally activities that you'll spend with your loved ones—and find excitement in them.

It's possible it will take you a long time to find something at least matching the excitement and joy of accomplishing more in your business, but in the end it will let you enjoy a more balanced and sustainable life.

Chapter 4: Four Toolsets to Develop Your Self-Discipline as an Entrepreneur

Self-discipline is the sum of empowering behaviors, traits, and habits that strengthen your self-command. In addition to the fundamental pieces of the puzzle we've already revealed, entrepreneurs need a few more tools to build self-discipline. In this chapter we'll cover them in detail grouped into four toolsets consisting of traits, habits, or mindset changes necessary to strengthen your resolve as an entrepreneur.

We'll discuss how and why these tools work as well as cover practical ways to implement them in your life. When you introduce them in your life, you'll benefit from a synergic effect that will generate long-term, unwavering self-discipline.

1. Dedication and Drive

Dedication means fully investing yourself in your business. Drive fuels the devotion to the process. Consistent use of these two inseparable tools is the most crucial difference between entrepreneurs who succeed in the long term and the ones who give up.

In his signature no-holds-barred writing style, successful entrepreneur and bestselling author MJ DeMarco writes in his book *The Millionaire Fastlane: Crack the Code to Wealth and Live Rich for a Lifetime,* "to hit the top of your game, business or otherwise, you have to eat, live, and shit your thing. If you're dabbling in ten different things, your results will be dabbling and unimpressive. Focus on one thing and do it in the most excellent way."[xxviii]

Dedication starts with a conscious decision to cut all possible escape routes and commit to one business idea until one of two things happens: it either becomes successful or it fails. There's no in-between, "dabbling into it" or "giving it a try."

Spreading your attention over more than one business idea at a time will dilute your persistence.

When you face obstacles with one of your businesses, it's tempting to close up shop and move on to another idea. Why would you fight for your first business if there's always the second one that—for now—isn't that troublesome? You don't have such a luxury when you run one business, and this ensures you'll give your best when you face setbacks instead of seeking the comfort of another business.

Oh, you say, but there are so many entrepreneurs who run multiple businesses!

People like Elon Musk and Richard Branson may run multiple businesses *now*, but they both started with just one venture and launched new businesses only when their previous projects no longer needed their active participation. Decades of experience, trustworthy teams of world-class employees, and virtually endless capital allow them to run multiple businesses. If you lack these resources, you'd better stick to one thing.

I strongly suggest giving a new project at least six months of your undivided attention. By committing all of your resources to one business you'll dramatically increase your chances of success and reduce the temptation to chase after the next shiny thing.

Once you commit to one business, dedicate yourself to it by establishing a consistent routine.

As a self-published author, I set for myself word count goals I have to achieve on a daily basis. I know that to maintain self-discipline my behavior has to be automated, so I don't wait for the muse to visit me. Instead, I follow Stephen King's advice: "Amateurs sit and wait for inspiration, the rest of us just get up and go to work."[xxix]

A strong work ethic is one of the most powerful allies of self-discipline and persistence. Establish a daily routine with one key task you absolutely must do before everything else. It's best if the task is quantifiable and repeatable, like writing a thousand words each day, calling thirty potential clients, or writing two hundred lines of code.

To maintain dedication to the process, you also need to fill your tank with the proper fuel: powerful drive or purpose.

As I write in my newsletter series on developing a process-oriented mindset (you'll get these emails if you sign up for my list by following a link you'll find in the beginning or at the end of the book):

"Most people would only *like to* become financially independent, and so they keep wishing for it for the rest of their lives. The ones who actually achieve the goal are the ones who don't merely desire it—they are the ones who absolutely need it in their lives and are willing to pay the price to achieve it. They're the ones willing to break through multiple bouts of depression and frustration, failures, and feeling like a recluse—all to make their dream come true."

That's the kind of drive you need in your entrepreneurial life to keep working on your dreams until they turn into reality. It's not about mere self-gratifying passion, though; it's about doing it because you *must* do it, fueled by the desire to chase mastery and provide value to the world.

Ryan Holiday, bestselling author of *Ego Is the Enemy*, posits, "Purpose is about pursuing something outside yourself as opposed to pleasuring yourself," and suggests that you should "make it about what you feel you *must* do and say, not what you care about and wish to be."[xxx]

Starting today, make your work more purposeful by chasing mastery and serving not only yourself, but primarily others. Remember prosocial and intrinsic motivation? The drive for mastery is one of the finest expressions of them.

2. Focus and Deliberation

Running two businesses at once is a recipe for distraction. It offers an easy way out of your troublesome business. Instead of fixing it, it's easier to call it quits and move on to another project, only to repeat the same mistake when you encounter obstacles on the new path.

However, distractions can also strike you if you're faithful to one business.

For instance, many people like to play at being an entrepreneur by designing business cards, a logo, or a website with all the trendy gizmos. They delude themselves by thinking this busywork is an important steppingstone to starting a business, when it should take a backseat. They distract themselves with irrelevant tasks instead of focusing on what's important—value creation.

That's why you need focus and deliberation in your life. These tools will help you uncover what's important *right now*.

Each time you're about to commit your resources to a task, ask yourself if it's really what you're *needing now*. Think in terms of smart work that produces results, not doing work for the sake of working. It might feel good to spend a few hours tweaking your business card, but in the end this action doesn't produce what your fledgling business needs the most—clients.

This simple habit of focused work will help you avoid applying self-discipline to low-impact tasks, and thus have more of it left for what's truly important.

And speaking of focus, another challenge is dealing with workplace distractions that negatively impact your productivity.

You're sitting in your office, working on an important task, and suddenly you get an email or somebody calls you. You reply to the message or finish the conversation. It's time to go back to work, but before you do it you decide to quickly check your Facebook page. You reply to a few messages, watch a new movie trailer your friend has just shared and comment on the travel pictures of another friend. You look at the clock and thirty minutes have just disappeared.

Distractions produce a chain reaction. Give into them once, and get ready to welcome several more distractions.

In his book *Your Brain at Work: Strategies for Overcoming Distraction, Regaining Focus, and Working Smarter All Day Long,* author David Rock writes, "One study found that office distractions eat an average 2.1 hours a day. Another study, published in October 2005, found that employees spent an average of eleven minutes on a project before being distracted. After an interruption it takes them twenty-five minutes to return to the original task, if they do at all."[xxxi]

It takes a lot of time to get back into the groove after you lose focus, and an average person loses focus many times during the workday. If you can't control distractions in your everyday life, you'll also struggle to control yourself.

The key to dealing with distractions is to acknowledge they'll happen and plan for them beforehand. You can't eliminate distractions altogether, but you can rein them in by doing these three things:

1. Work on the most important task when you're least likely to be interrupted, ideally in the morning. Even if you get distracted at some point later during your day, at least you've already done the most important task.

In his article for PsychologyToday.com, author David Rock recommends to "do your deeper thinking work in the morning while you still have the ability to control your attention."[xxxii]

I like to wake up at 5:00 AM to do my most important work because the house is quiet, my mind is fresh, and nobody else is up yet.

2. Avoid distractions by working in a place where you're least likely to be interrupted. It might be trendy to work in a co-working space or a café, but you'll do your best work in a quiet place where it's only you and the task at hand. As an entrepreneur, you probably have freedom to work wherever you want. Choose seclusion.

In her interview with FastCompany.com, interruption scientist Gloria Mark suggests that her personal best ways to avoid distractions are to work at home (to avoid the distracting office environment) and limit her web usage to twice per day.[xxxiii]

Heed this advice by creating a private home office space and disconnecting from the Internet if you don't need it for work. Consider using browser add-ons that allow you to block specific sites for a specific period of time.

3. Be mindful and take breaks whenever you feel your attention slipping away. Consider following the

Pomodoro approach in which you work for twenty-five minutes, do a five-minute break and continue with another round of twenty-five minutes.[xxxiv]

Additionally, consider meditation as a training tool to sharpen your focus. The more often you engage in an activity that consumes your entire focus, the better you'll get at maintaining the same level of attention when working. If you don't find meditation particularly useful or you don't like it, consider other types of meditative-like activities such as:

- Listening mindfully to music,

- Practicing yoga or tai chi,

- Journaling,

- Other non-standard types of meditation like walking meditation, gazing meditation, breathing meditation or gratitude meditation (I've covered all of these alternatives to meditation in my book *Daily Self-Discipline: Everyday Habits and Exercises to Build Self-Discipline and Achieve Your Goals*).

3. Decisiveness and Selectivity

As an entrepreneur, you'll frequently find yourself in difficult situations where you won't be able to make an informed decision.

You could choose to make no decision, but even that is a decision. And in the end, it's the worst decision you can make because then you let things happen to you instead of choosing what to do and assuming the responsibility for the outcome.

Self-discipline can't thrive in an environment where you let things happen to you because self-discipline is *also* a decision to choose delayed gratification over instant rewards. Entrepreneurship is about being proactive and taking control, not reacting to what's happening to you.

How do you become a more decisive and selective person?

It all starts with understanding that making decisions consumes energy. The more decisions you make, the lower their quality. In psychology, this phenomenon is called *decision fatigue.*[xxxv] Decision fatigue can also lead to *decision avoidance* wherein you avoid decisions entirely.[xxxvi]

President Barack Obama once said, "You'll see I wear only gray or blue suits. I'm trying to pare down decisions. I don't want to make decisions about what I'm eating or wearing. Because I have too many other decisions to make." He then also added: "You need to focus your decision-making energy. You need to routinize yourself. You can't be going through the day distracted by trivia."[xxxvii]

There's no denying that the number of decisions a president must take goes well beyond the quota of a typical person. Consequently, I'd say he probably knows how to manage his decision-making energy, don't you think?

Not dealing with trivia by simplifying your everyday choices will free up energy needed to make important decisions.

Get rid of clothes you no longer wear, or invest only in classics that always work with each other. Buy and eat similar foods to simplify your nutritional habits. Go with the first thing that comes to your mind when you're forced to make a trivial decision like choosing between the flavors of sauce when eating out.

Reduce or eliminate trivial decisions from your life, but be selective when it comes to key decisions with long-term consequences.

When I decided to translate my books into other languages, I went through dozens of applications to find the right translator and editor. I could have been less picky, but I knew that the task was too important to cut corners.

Apply selectivity in the same way. Don't settle for mediocrity or make hasty decisions if there's a lot at stake. As for trivial choices, don't waste your time on them; make a quick decision.

4. Determination and Self-Trust

Scientists refer to determination as a positive emotional feeling that pushes you toward action despite difficulties.[xxxviii] It makes you more persistent and improves your ability to cope with problems.

As an entrepreneur, you'll face setbacks on a regular basis. There won't be anyone to handle them for you. If you're unused to walls frequently popping up on your journey toward success, at first you might feel the temptation to give up. The opposite reaction—determination—will help you focus on the solutions: climb the wall, destroy it, or go around it.

In this sense, determination is about having an internal locus of control and the belief that you control your life, and it's you—not the external factors like luck, other people, or the economy—who can change it.[xxxix]

A person with external locus of control won't be able to deal with the wall. They would stare at it thinking "they" (whoever this is) want to keep them away from success and there's nothing they can do but accept their fate.

To develop an internal locus of control, stop blaming the world around you. Accept equal responsibility for every success and failure that you experience.

Such constant reinforcement will encourage you to approach every difficulty with an action-oriented mindset instead of complaining about external factors.

Secondly, develop your self-efficacy, which is the strength of your belief in your abilities and how likely you perceive yourself successfully performing a given task or achieving a goal.[xl]

In my book *Confidence: How to Overcome Your Limiting Beliefs and Achieve Your Goals*, I cover five fundamental rules to develop a strong sense of self-efficacy. They are:

1. Set goals slightly above your ability so you can consistently stretch your comfort zone and get used to bigger and bigger challenges. In business, it might be starting with small investments and slowly increasing your risk threshold.

2. Break goals into smaller pieces and simplify them to avoid being overwhelmed. Starting a business sounds like a big undertaking, but when you break it into small tasks, it's more manageable. Then you'll be more likely to feel determined instead of discouraged.

3. Focus on the big picture to think in terms of strategies instead of tactics. As an entrepreneur, your

primary goal is to make sales. Everything else is background, especially for a person just starting out. As we've already covered, focus on key actions instead of busying yourself with things that might feel good but don't generate results.

4. Reframe obstacles so you think of them as reasons to keep going instead of reasons to give up. As American professor Randy Pausch said, "The brick walls are there for a reason. The brick walls are not there to keep us out. The brick walls are there to give us a chance to show how badly we want something. Because the brick walls are there to stop the people who don't want it badly enough. They're there to stop the other people."[xli]

5. Take control over your life so you acknowledge that what happens in your life is the direct result of your actions. This goes back to developing an internal locus of control.

In practice, as long as you vow not to stop until you make your business work, you'll develop determination naturally, just like you naturally get stronger if you regularly lift heavy weights.

Three Key Actionable Implications

The three most important actions you can take to implement advice from this chapter in your life are:

1. Dedicate Yourself

If you want to build powerful self-discipline, you absolutely must be dedicated to your business and its growth. This includes following an established routine to help you stick to the process and not spreading yourself thin by working on a few unrelated projects at once.

Starting today, vow to develop unconditional dedication to the process of building your business. Give yourself at least six months (and ideally a year or more) to focus on your business and forget about any new, alluring business ideas. Develop one key routine that you'll follow every business day (like calling a specific number of prospects or producing a specific quantity of a product) and don't deviate from it no matter what.

2. Work Smart and Be Focused

Working smart and properly managing your resources instead of spinning your wheels and being wasteful will help you achieve better results more quickly. This in turn will reduce your risk of giving up due to a lack of persistence or self-discipline.

Get the most important tasks done as early as possible or whenever you can best avoid interruptions. Additionally, come to terms with the fact that distractions *will* happen, so it's better to work in short bursts and schedule distractions for your short breaks.

Consider meditation or engaging in a similar meditative-like type of activity that will help you declutter your mind and single-task.

Be mindful when choosing new tasks to perform. It's easy to fall into the trap of doing things just because it feels good to complete them even if they don't serve any specific purpose. Assume that your self-discipline is a limited resource and avoid the wastefulness of doing unnecessary tasks.

Review the tasks you do on a regular basis and ask yourself which are key to do and which aren't necessary. Reduce the time spent on less important tasks or eliminate them altogether from your schedule.

Don't forget that decisions also take energy. The more time you spend making unimportant decisions the harder it is to make the right important decisions. Reduce the number of trivial decisions as much as you can and be selective regarding important choices that can have long-term repercussions.

3. Learn to Trust Yourself

Entrepreneurs often doubt themselves. This can lead to a weak resolve and decision avoidance.

Learn how to trust yourself by constantly stepping outside your comfort zone and trying things that are increasingly difficult. Starting today, every day try to do at least one thing that scares you or makes you feel uncomfortable.

Additionally, break each challenge into smaller steps to avoid getting overwhelmed. If you have some big goals, break them into smaller stepping stones.

Last but most definitely not least, think about the big picture—long-term strategies rather than short-term tactics, big changes rather than small tweaks.

Assess your current approach and ask yourself if you're primarily focused on the little things or the more important long-term outlook.

FOUR TOOLSETS TO DEVELOP YOUR SELF-DISCIPLINE AS AN ENTREPRENEUR: QUICK RECAP

1. Dedication to the process is the first fundamental key of self-discipline for an entrepreneur. If you don't give your full, undivided focus to your business, you'll struggle. Long-term persistence comes from the commitment to staying faithful to one business.

2. Strengthen your dedication by developing a powerful drive to become the best at what you do and focusing on the value you're adding to the world. When you start feeling like you *must* do it, you become unstoppable.

3. Be deliberate. Whenever you're about to spend your time or energy on a big task, ask yourself it it's necessary. Some entrepreneurs often work for the sense of superficial achievement rather than to get real-world results. Think about smart work and results, not mindless hard work and busyness for the sake of busyness.

4. Handle distractions by acknowledging they'll happen and planning accordingly—for instance, by working in 25-minute sprints. A lack of focus will lead to mediocre results, and mediocre results won't lead to the success you're seeking.

5. A decisive person is a person who makes and acts on their decisions instead of waiting for things to happen to them. This characterizes the proactive mindset vital to every entrepreneur. Manage your decision-making energy by reducing the number of unimportant decisions you make on a daily basis. In addition to that, be selective and think carefully when making important decisions.

6. Assume responsibility for everything that happens in your life and practice determination by constantly stepping outside your comfort zone. Your ability to cope with problems and failure will grow naturally as a result of challenging yourself.

Chapter 5: The Most Common Challenges Facing People Who Want to Start a Business

One of the most common problems faced by people wishing to start a business is exactly this—*wishing*. The term I like to use for a person with this challenge is "wantrepreneur," which UrbanDictionary defines as "someone who thinks about being an entrepreneur or starting a business but never gets started."[xlii]

Wantrepreneurs either don't start businesses at all or pretend they're entrepreneurs by running little money-making ventures that are doomed to fail, often built in accordance with bad advice from "make money online" gurus.

We've already discussed that commitment is one of the most important things you need to achieve success in business. In addition to that (and other traits and habits we've discussed so far), here are five more reasons why people are wantrepreneurs—and how to overcome them.

1. Fear

If you've always relied on the paycheck from your employer, you can find it scary that as an entrepreneur you only get paid when you get results. This fear can become so paralyzing that you keep dreaming about starting a business for years but never do it because you're afraid you'll starve or lose your house.

I would love to give you an exact step-by-step process to overcome fear, but unfortunately it doesn't exist. Just like you're never going to be one hundred percent ready to be a parent, you're never going to be fully prepared to become an entrepreneur. The only way in which you can make the transition is to actually start your business.

It doesn't mean that you need to go all-in right away and give in a notice. Working on your business as a side thing at first is a good way to break through fear. This will allow you to gain some initial momentum without the risk of ending up in a bad financial situation, which is a particularly important consideration if you have to provide for your family.

If you can't imagine yourself making money from your own venture, start small with something simple like:

- Buying a used item like a phone or a car, cleaning and/or fixing it, taking some good pictures of it, and selling it with a small markup. Alternatively, buy such things in bulk and sell them individually for a higher price. I used to buy music CDs in bulk and sell them individually. It was a good experience to learn how to run a little business without committing a lot of money or time to it.

- Benefiting from the "gig economy" by offering your services as a freelancer on websites like Upwork (you can even offer the same services you perform for your current employer), becoming a driver at one of the ridesharing startups like Uber, or teaching English (or other languages you speak) through sites like Italki. I used to write articles for various clients. While I wouldn't call it a "proper" business—it was more of a job, albeit with me as a boss—it still taught me many useful things I later used as an entrepreneur.

- Selling things you've made with your hands through crafts marketplaces like Etsy. This can easily grow into a full-fledged business.

Making even a small amount of money outside of a regular job will develop the confidence that you can make money on your own. This will help you transition from a wantrepreneur into an entrepreneur.

Even if you fail with your first little ventures—and let's be straight, it *will* happen—you'll learn how to handle failure and keep going. All entrepreneurs have a highly developed ability to deal with failure. If you want to achieve success, prepare to acquire this skill, too.

2. Perfectionism

Many perfectionists put off things for later in fear they won't be able to achieve perfect results.

Guess what… You will *never* achieve perfect results in anything new to you.

It doesn't mean you shouldn't start, though.

When I started writing books, I experimented with numerous genres, including fiction. The stories were embarrassing, but I knew that I had to release them in order to get real-world feedback. I was surprised when instead of 1-star reviews I received 3-star, 4-star, and even some 5-star reviews. People actually *liked* my books, the very same ones I considered embarrassing.

Since then, I've improved my writing skills and refined my approach. If it weren't for this initial experience and exposing myself to criticism, I wouldn't be where I am today.

As a perfectionist you most likely have unrealistic standards. Fortunately, as you can learn from my story, what you think about the results of your work probably won't match the perception of your market that will be happy to use what you've created.

If you're a wantrepreneur because you're afraid you won't do a good job, assume your first product or service *will* suck and do it anyway. More often than not it won't be nearly as bad as you think. In the end, doing it anyway is the only effective solution to escape the perfectionism-related inaction.

Please note that perfectionism also applies to waiting for perfect circumstances. For instance, many entrepreneurs believe they shouldn't start a business if they can't get financing. Guess what... You can always do *something*, even if all you have is five bucks in your wallet.

When I was working on my software business, I didn't have enough money to develop the entire application. Consequently, I started small with a rough minimum viable product (a barebones product with the most essential features early adopters needed) and raised money directly from my clients.

Ingenuity can go a long way if you stop waiting for the stars to align in your favor and act anyway.

Another expression of perfectionism is spending countless hours studying books about entrepreneurship but never implementing the advice in the real world.

It's good to educate yourself about the basics of entrepreneurship, but true business education starts when you launch a business. Only then the concepts covered in the books you've read will start to make sense, and you'll also be able to filter out the advice that's not applicable in your situation.

3. The All-or-Nothing Mentality

Another common reason why people keep wishing about entrepreneurship but never make it a reality is because they think in terms of all or nothing.

Either they'll start this big, sexy Silicon Valley startup that everyone will talk about or they won't start anything at all. To them, building a minimum viable product isn't enough.

It's either a glamorous, "never done before" invention or nothing—certainly not a slightly improved version of an existing product instead.

It's either a huge retail store right away or nothing. Testing the idea with a small online store isn't good enough.

It's easy to see that the only outcome of such a mentality is doing nothing. A person thinking in terms of all or nothing will wait for the right circumstances (that won't happen) or waste any

98

opportunities coming their way because they won't produce the instantly big results they need.

Yet again, the most powerful solution is to take action and do something anyway. Have you noticed a common theme?

If you're new to business, I strongly suggest starting with something small and easy, just to gain some experience and confidence.

Thinking big is admirable, but if you have no practical experience in the field you'd like to dominate, your chances of launching a big company without any prior business experience are nil. Instead, first dip your toe in the water, get a feel for how realistic your plans are, and adjust accordingly.

Before I started taking tennis classes, I had thought it would take me a few classes at most to learn how to play properly. Little did I know that it takes more like a year or two to master the game. If I had thought in terms of "all or nothing" I would have given up after the first few classes.

In this sense, business is like tennis. Your all-or-nothing mentality can tempt you to have unrealistic expectations that discredit all kinds of small achievements and ruin your motivation.

Start small. Slowly stretch your comfort zone. Accept the fact that it's highly unlikely that your first venture will take off or you'll grow a big business right away. However, without taking these first steps you'll never achieve those huge goals you have for yourself.

4. Making Excuses

People make excuses because:

1. They don't have enough confidence or problem-solving skills, or their perception of their abilities makes them think they'll be unable to deal with the reality of running a business. We've covered this one when talking about fear.

2. They don't want success badly enough but need to rationalize their inaction. The problem isn't the excuses they give but their weak motivation.

3. They worry too much or tend to make mountains out of molehills. Their excuses are either irrelevant or not nearly as difficult to deal with as they think.

When it comes to the second reason why people make excuses—not wanting success badly enough—it all comes down to your mentality.

If the only reason why you want to start a business is because you want to make money and get rich, with no further thought as to why you need the money, it will be hard to start and even more difficult to keep going.

We've already covered it in the first chapter. Extrinsic motivation is helpful, but it can't stand on its own legs without the support of intrinsic motivation and ideally prosocial motivation as well.

If you've been procrastinating about starting a business for months or years, perhaps it's time to reconsider your motivators. Millions of people around the world want to be millionaires. In an ideal world, maybe a small percentage of them actually take consistent action. These are the ones who are driven so much that it feels like a life or death matter—and these are the people who make it happen.

If you make excuses because you worry too much or tend to make mountains out of molehills, it's time to sit down, deconstruct your worries, and realize that millions of people have dealt with the same issues and have managed just fine.

The problems you imagine to be so overpowering are often in reality small hurdles you can easily jump over. As long as their negative consequences won't have a long-term impact on you, why worry about them so much?

For instance, let's assume that you're putting off launching your business because you're afraid you don't know how to design a website, set up a company, or use a merchant account.

Are these fears legitimate? What's the worst that can happen if you design a bad website, fail to file some paperwork, or can't manage to open a proper merchant account?

If you design a bad website, you can always redesign it. Or instead of designing it yourself again, you can figure out how to download a free template and look professional despite having zero knowledge about website design. In the worst case, you risk embarrassment.

Unless you're starting a business in an extremely regulated industry, the risk of neglecting paperwork is minuscule. Even if you do fail to file some paperwork and get fined, it will most likely only happen once. Consider the fine a learning experience.

How about the inability to open a merchant account? It's not necessary to accept payments. You can start with PayPal, Stripe, or any other similar credit card processor. Nothing to risk here.

Deconstruct your worries in the same way and realize that as long as the negative consequences are one-off and won't have a lasting impact on your life, the risks are low and your excuses aren't legitimate.

5. Entitlement and Consumer Mentality

One of the worst mindsets that will prevent you from achieving entrepreneurial success is entitlement mentality: believing that everything should be given to you just because you exist.

Entrepreneurial individuals with such a mindset often busy themselves with various short-term moneymaking schemes. They never launch a proper business providing real value to their clients because their only concern is how to make as much money as quickly and easily as possible.

In this type of wantrepreneurship you're at least taking action, but it's the wrong kind of action, focused on making quick money and fleeting streams of revenue. You don't procrastinate when it comes to taking action like other wantrepreneurs, but you postpone starting a legitimate business.

There are countless "authors" in the self-publishing industry who entered it only because they had heard it could be profitable. Instead of coming up with a way to serve their readers in the best way possible, they mass-produce low-quality books in the hot genres.

The end result is easy to predict: discouraged by unsatisfying sales of their low-quality books, they move on to another moneymaking scheme.

A cure to this problem is simple: whenever you catch yourself thinking about making quick money with an unsustainable business model that doesn't benefit anyone but you, resist the temptation to do it and think about something more legitimate.

Entitlement mentality is a cousin to consumer mentality. People often remain wantrepreneurs because they start a business thinking in terms of what they can get out of the business (thinking like a consumer) instead of what they can offer to the world (thinking like a producer).

These are the kind of people who buy into hot trends and industries even when they have zero experience with them, aren't willing to learn, and don't care about providing real value.

To remedy this situation, honestly assess your unique skills, traits, and whatever else you can bring to the table. I've always been a writer, so when I first heard about self-publishing I realized it could be a perfect fit for my personal skillset. What are your marketable abilities and how you can combine them to start a business and offer value to the world?

Actionable Implication

In this chapter I'll leave you with just one actionable implication. It supersedes everything else and it's the only real-world solution to overcome wantrepreneurship. It's:

1. Take Action, Commit, and Tweak Things Until They Fall into Place

Okay, technically we could break it into three actionable implications, but in reality it's all one process.

Taking action, which can be as simple as talking with your potential customers and offering them your early solution, will help you overcome inertia and gain initial momentum. If you don't take actions that provide real value to others, you'll forever remain in the wantrepreneurial dreamland.

Today, perform at least one action that will produce a direct result of helping someone. You don't need to charge for it; many businesses start with people performing a service for others or giving away a product for free as a loss leader.

It doesn't end with taking action, though. When you finally get some initial results, it's time to commit to your business idea for at least six months. Without committing yourself to the process you'll end up chasing after the next shiny thing.

I strongly suggest finding a way to hold yourself accountable. For instance, you can give your friend a substantial amount of money and tell them to spend it as they wish if you don't stick to your business idea for an agreed upon period of time. Public accountability such as creating a progress thread on a forum about entrepreneurship or joining a mastermind group can help, too.

The last step, but most definitely not least, is to keep tweaking things until they fall into place, regardless of how many failures you'll experience along the way. This phase is what differentiates successful entrepreneurs from those who give up.

When I started in the self-publishing industry, taking action—writing and publishing my first book—was the first step. Committing to the industry—vowing not to try anything else until I would make it work—was the second step. Lastly, I kept testing various niches, writing styles, and marketing approaches until they fell into place and I released my first bestseller, *How to Build Self-Discipline*.

Don't just read this passage and forget about it. Test your business idea today and gain momentum. All you need to escape the dreary world of wantrepreneurs and join the exciting world of entrepreneurs is *action*.

THE MOST COMMON CHALLENGES FACING PEOPLE WHO WANT TO START A BUSINESS: QUICK RECAP

1. Wantrepreneurship, or wishing to start a business but never doing it, is one of the most common challenges of new entrepreneurs. Five most common reasons why they resort to wishing, but never taking action are: fear, perfectionism, the all or nothing mentality, making excuses, and entitlement and consumer mentality.

2. A fear of starting a new business, or rather, the perceived negative consequences of a failure, can paralyze you so much that you'll dream about becoming self-employed for years but never take action. To handle this problem, start small with a business idea that won't require much capital, time, and involvement. Slowly stretch your comfort zone until you feel ready to transition to full-time entrepreneurship. There's no need to go all in right away.

3. Perfectionism is another reason for wantrepreneurship. If you're worried that your

business won't be perfect right away, you'll forever postpone launching anything. To deal with this problem, assume that your first product *will* suck and do it anyway. At some point, every one of the most successful entrepreneurs in history was a novice.

4. The all-or-nothing mentality is a mindset in which you either launch a world-changing business or nothing. Unfortunately, rarely, if ever, will a new entrepreneur launch a business that achieves much success right away. It takes years to acquire real-world business experience. Get rid of your unrealistic expectations by starting a small business. Your first venture most likely won't be your lifetime occupation, anyway.

5. Wantrepreneurs often make excuses. They do it because they're afraid, because they lack proper motivation, or because they worry too much and tend to make mountains out of molehills.

If you make excuses because you're afraid, revisit how to escape wantrepreneurship if you feel fear. Slowly stretch your comfort zone to destroy the spell your excuses have on you.

If you make excuses because you lack motivation, it's time to revisit your reason why and add stronger intrinsic and prosocial motivators. If your sole motivator is a Ferrari, you'll be unlikely to make all the necessary sacrifices and keep pushing. (That is, unless you love Ferraris over everything else in your life.)

If you make excuses because you worry too much, deconstruct your worries and ask yourself about the potential negative effects of your anxieties coming true. Will they cause a once-off problem? Will it really affect your life that much or will you be able to carry on right away? More often than not, the problems you imagine in your head are only small hurdles.

6. You can't approach your business as a consumer, let alone feel you're entitled to success. Think of business as a vehicle that can help you serve others, and as an extension help yourself. People who focus on money over everything else, rather than thinking how they can create value with their personal

skills, are the ones who fail with their money-making schemes and give up.

Chapter 6: Common Self-Discipline Challenges for Experienced Entrepreneurs

Experienced entrepreneurs may no longer deal with some of the most common troubles of new entrepreneurs, but it doesn't mean their problems are gone. More often than not, the old challenges are replaced with a new set that can be as tricky as the growing pains.

In this chapter we'll discuss these problems and solutions to them. Even if you have a few years of business experience, you most likely have dealt with, or are still dealing with, some of these difficulties. However, they too can be solved, and it's crucial you do so if you want to remain a successful entrepreneur for the rest of your life.

Resting on Your Laurels

Experienced entrepreneurs often succumb to the temptation to take it easy. It's understandable that when you achieve some of your goals, you'll lose the original hunger that made you maintain strong work ethic. However, taking it too easy often leads to a slippery slope.

Just like your muscles require regular workouts to maintain their strength and mass, so does your self-discipline need a consistent "workout" to stay on top of your game.

Even the most successful entrepreneurs continue to push forward because they know that if they don't continuously challenge themselves, they'll lose their edge.

In his interview with NBC News, Steve Jobs said: "I think if you do something and it turns out pretty good, then you should go do something else wonderful, not dwell on it for too long. Just figure out what's next."[xliii]

By all means, go on a vacation or relax for a period of time if you've achieved a huge success, but resist the temptation to think that now you're set for life. Success is not a given—it's a continuous process of maintaining good habits and consistent action-taking.

I know a person who has gone from a successful, almost passive business, to making zero income overnight, just because he thought he had it made and neglected his business for too long. He's learned his lesson and rebounded, but I'm sure you'd rather not find yourself in a similar situation.

Here are three practical suggestions that will help you avoid resting on your laurels and strengthen your resolve to keep pushing despite achieving your long-term goals:

1. Challenge Yourself

Entrepreneurs thrive on challenges and constant growth. If you've achieved your original business goals and stopped stepping outside your comfort zone, it's no wonder you don't feel like pushing harder.

To get excited about new opportunities and challenge yourself, you can:

- Create new products or services. Experiment with different types of products and services. For me as an author, writing one book after another can get tedious. To battle the lack of stimuli I started creating video courses like my course *How to Build Self-Discipline* and audio courses like my course *Supercharge Your Self-Discipline.*

- Enter a new market. Sell your products in another country or to a different group of clients. I translate my books into foreign languages.

- Expand your business into another, related industry—ideally one that converges with your primary industry. For instance, if you sell consulting services to startups, it's likely they'd also buy dedicated software from you.

When you put yourself in a position of a newbie again, you'll feel a renewed sense of challenge to motivate you to keep growing your business.

Sit down, grab a notepad or create a new document on your computer, and make a list of possible new products, services, markets, industries, or any other improvements you can make to your business to get yourself excited about new opportunities.

2. Reward Yourself

Many entrepreneurs rest on their laurels because they accomplished their original financial goals. Adding more numbers to their bank accounts is no longer enough of a motivation, so they slack off.

Obviously, the first step would be to come up with intrinsic and prosocial motivators, but you can start with something simpler—namely, reward yourself to translate the virtual meaning of money in your bank account into something real.

Spending money on things that can significantly improve your happiness for a long period of time might be just enough to remind you that you've been working hard on your business for a reason, and this reason isn't some digits in your bank account but a real improvement of the quality of your life.

I'm frugal by nature. This tendency sometimes negatively impacts my motivation because I feel reluctant to spend money on things that would reignite the spark inside me, such as traveling.

For a period of time I lacked the motivation to work. A few days before writing this paragraph I convinced myself not to be such a miser and bought tickets for a two-week overseas trip.

As if by magic, my motivation returned overnight—not because money spent on the trip made a big dent in my savings and I felt the need to replenish them, but because it transformed the virtual feeling of money in my bank account into an experience that happened in the real world.

If you haven't yet rewarded yourself for your success with something more substantial than mere numbers in your bank account, consider doing so.

I highly suggest spending it on experiences like travel or quality time with friends and family. Numerous studies[xliv, xlv, xlvi, xlvii] show that experiential purchases improve happiness more and for a longer period of time than material purchases.

A new car gets old in a few months. A trip to the Hawaii with your significant other will stay with you forever. When you get back recharged and relaxed, it's highly likely you'll *want* to stop being complacent and challenge yourself yet again.

3. Start a New Business

If your business no longer requires your personal involvement, consider starting a new business. Now that you have a steady stream of income and a lot of business experience, running multiple businesses is no longer such a bad proposition as for a new entrepreneur.

The challenge and excitement of building something from the ground up has the potential to resurrect your entrepreneurial energy and work ethic.

The more unrelated the new business will be, the more stimulating the experience will be. You'll get rid of boredom and feel excited again. As successful entrepreneur Neil Patel wrote in his article for Entrepreneur.com titled "Why You Should Never Start Just One Business," if you keep starting new companies, you'll never live another boring day in your life.

He also pointed out that starting multiple businesses keeps you fresh. In his words: "Every time you start a new company, you learn something new. In my entrepreneurial pursuits, I've launched businesses in industries that I knew nothing about going into. Learning is half the fun of doing, and keeps your mind sharp and your skills fresh."[xlviii]

Keeping your mind sharp is the opposite of dangerous complacency that makes you lose the will to grow.

Last but not least, Neil argued, "One of the worst things that you can do with your experience is to let it waste away. Experience is meant to be used, shared and acted upon—not stifled."

And that sums up well why resting on your laurels is not a good idea. Relax from time to time and enjoy the fruits of your labor. However, don't deprive the world—and yourself—of the gift of your experience. Stay sharp and keep growing.

Burnout

Entrepreneurs who find themselves stuck in a rut often lose the willingness to continue working on their businesses. And as we've already learned, a lack of enthusiasm kills motivation.

My personal experience suggests that you can't force your way through a burnout. It won't disappear overnight. More often than not, it's been brewing inside you for a long time. However, it doesn't mean you should coast along and expect it will resolve itself with no action on your part.

The first, crucial action to battle burnout is to take a break. Don't delude yourself thinking you'll make the burnout go away with more work. It's like trying to heal an injury by performing the same activity that has caused it. Just like in sports, it's time to take a break and let your body (and mind) heal, not aggravate the injury further.

At a minimum, take an entire week off. Get away from your everyday routine as much as your obligations allow you. I'm partial to traveling, but it can be anything that breaks your routine and puts distance between you and your business.

During the break, nurture yourself. Eat healthy, sleep as much as you need, unplug, occupy yourself with pleasant activities. It's about resetting yourself, so no real work should be done during this time. If you can't leave your business to itself, at least find a way to work as little as possible. This is not a time to think about the health of your business—your well-being should be the priority.

If you've been suffering from burnout for a longer period of time, don't expect a weeklong break to bring you back to top form, though. It might take a month, two, or three. You can't revert years of bad eating habits with a week of a diet, and you can't deal with a long-term burnout with a seven-day break.

Once you return from your vacation, you still might not exactly feel like working, but at least your mind and body will be recharged. It's time to gently stretch your resolve by doing *anything*.

Successful entrepreneur, programmer, and writer Derek Sivers suggests in his article "When You're Extremely Un-Motivated" to start doing things you've been putting off for years but need to be done. As a result, you'll move from doing nothing to doing something, and that will eventually make you feel like doing something important again.[xlix]

This little trick is a good way to transition from the recovery period into slowly reinserting yourself into your previous routine. Alternatively, start with simple, quick tasks and slowly stretch your comfort zone until you get back into the groove.

If you suffer from burnout that borders on depression, please talk with a professional. Deeper psychological issues require therapy, not a self-help book.

Saying "Yes" to Too Many Things

Saying "yes" to too many things is another common challenge of seasoned entrepreneurs. As we've already discussed, launching a new product or starting a new business can help if you need a kick in the pants. However, as with everything, moderation is the key. You don't want to bite off more than you can chew.

Oftentimes, once your business starts running more smoothly, you'll feel the temptation to start new projects you've always wanted to do. This can be a good thing until you fill your entire workday with work and lose balance.

The goal you've worked so hard to reach—building a successful business that will give you the freedom to do what you want—then leads you to even more work, more responsibilities, and even less time for yourself.

Deciding to capitalize on my experience as a self-published author, I launched as a side project a service helping fellow writers get honest reviews of their books.

Unfortunately, as weeks passed I started spending more and more time and energy on my secondary business at the expense of writing.

When I realized that I was spreading myself too thin, I sold my service business. I regained clarity and took my self-publishing company to the next level.

Saying "yes" to a new project was easy. Eliminating it from my life took several weeks. The experience taught me that side projects can quickly devour your main business—and if you don't realize it soon enough, they can cannibalize it.

Prevention is easier than cure. Think long and hard before you take on new responsibilities that can be difficult to eliminate from your life later on. I suggest following these three simple rules:

1. One Demanding, Active Role at a Time

This rule alone will save you a lot of problems. If you're thinking about starting a secondary project, do so only if your primary business can grow without your direct involvement. If your absence will affect it negatively, don't take on more responsibilities.

If you have systems in place and/or employees who manage the everyday operation of the business, and are able to grow it without your active involvement, you're free to work on a new project. Otherwise, find a way to extract yourself from the business before you think about new responsibilities.

2. Be an Investor, Not an Entrepreneur

One of the biggest mistakes I made with my service business was that I had assumed the primary role in it instead of approaching it as an investor. If I had hired a person whose task would be to grow the company under my guidance, I wouldn't have gotten so entangled in the business as I did.

If you're thinking about starting a new project, look at it like an investor. Can it run and grow with you as a person overseeing the operation instead of being the one doing the work? Can you develop processes that will minimize the amount of your personal, active involvement?

If you can't, chances are the business will soon dominate your entire day. If you're ready for it, by all means do so. If you want to run it as a side project, though, reconsider the idea.

It doesn't mean that you shouldn't start a new business if it can't run on autopilot from day one. A growing business always requires at least some personal involvement, but there's a difference between assuming the role of an owner who provides guidance and actively involved CEO who manages everything.

3. Think in the Long Term

Last but not least, don't dedicate yourself to any new projects without having an exit strategy— whether you want to eventually sell the business, automatize it, or hand it over to a manager. Failing to plan for the long term carries a risk of taking too much on your shoulders without the ability to throw the weight away quickly.

I was lucky that I created my service business to be sellable from the start. If I hadn't done so, I would have had a harder time eliminating it from my life, or I would have had to assume the losses and close up shop instead of selling it, losing all that I invested in it at the time.

Be particularly careful when it comes to long-term obligations like long contracts, big purchases necessary for the business, or hiring full-time employees. Such burdens can entrap you and turn your life into a nightmare when you decide you want to get out.

Three Key Actionable Implications

Here are three practical implications for dealing with common challenges of more seasoned entrepreneurs:

1. Reignite Excitement

Accomplishing all of your goals and the resulting boredom can make you rest on your laurels. Slacking off for too long will make you lose habits that have made you successful. If you've been resting on your laurels for too long, it's time to set a new challenge and make the business exciting for you again.

Think about a new product or service to launch. Consider expanding into other markets or industries. Lastly, if your business no longer requires your active personal involvement, consider launching a new venture.

If you're resting on your laurels because you lack the hunger to keep going after achieving all your long-term financial objectives, reward yourself with a nice experience that will transform the numbers in your bank account into something real and inspiring. Even a short trip can be enough to motivate you to get back to work so you can have more such trips in the future.

2. Take a Break

To handle a burnout, a long break is not merely recommended—it's a must.

If you feel like throwing up when you think about work, it's time to unplug, go on a vacation, and stay as far away as possible from business duties.

Don't feel guilty that you're not working or that you'll lose your work ethic. At this point, what's important is to regain mental health, not concern yourself about self-discipline.

If you can afford it and your obligations don't restrict your options, go ahead now and book a trip somewhere for at least a week. An ideal destination is a foreign country that will provide you with new stimuli and help you take your mind off work. If you can't just pack your things and travel, focus on daily self-care. Get enough sleep, put your diet in order, exercise, engage in your hobbies, and spend time with people you love.

3. De-Clutter Your Business Life

Make an assessment of your business responsibilities. Ask yourself which ones you can maintain in the long term and which ones add a lot of work but bring little in terms of benefits.

Then come up with ways to eliminate unnecessary responsibilities and reprioritize the ones that should take the driving seat.

COMMON SELF-DISCIPLINE CHALLENGES FOR EXPERIENCED ENTREPRENEURS: QUICK RECAP

1. Seasoned entrepreneurs can feel the temptation to rest on their laurels, thinking that they no longer have to make an effort to improve. While it's fine to celebrate success, it can be harmful to your long-term results if you take your business for granted and slip into bad habits.

2. The three main ways to deal with resting on your laurels are: setting new challenges by creating new products and services or entering new markets and industries, rewarding yourself (if you've been taking it easy because of the lack of motivation), and starting a new business (if you need a new challenge). Whenever you find yourself being too complacent, remind yourself that taking things for granted never ends well, particularly in business.

3. Burnout is another common challenge facing experienced entrepreneurs. If you're stuck in a rut, escape it by taking a long break. Spend it traveling, nurturing yourself by maintaining healthy habits, and

engaging in hobbies and activities that make you feel good. Push aside guilt for not working and recharge your batteries.

When you feel rested up, slowly stretch yourself by doing little tasks that will take you from inactivity to doing *something*, even if it isn't anything particularly urgent or important.

4. Saying "yes" to too many things can lead to overwhelm and exhaustion because of all the responsibilities you have to shoulder.

The key thing to remember about spreading yourself too thin is that it's easy to say "yes," but hard to say "no more" once you've taken on the new obligation. For this reason, it's crucial to become extremely careful and conscious when considering starting any new projects.

To avoid one-hundred-hour workweeks, follow three simple rules:

1. Have no more than one active, demanding role in a business. If you're a CEO of one company, don't start another company until your primary business can grow without you.

2. Think like an investor instead of a businessperson. If you have one business and want to start another as a side project, structure it from the start like a proper company instead of a one-man operation. The goal is to work *on* the company instead of working *in* the company.

3. Have an exit strategy. Don't start a new project just because it will be fun. Ponder on potential future opportunities to exit the business in case you'll no longer want to spend your energy on it or when it will start to distract you from other priorities too much.

Chapter 7: Frequently Asked Questions Related to Self-Discipline

The questions I'm about to answer come from my readers who have shared with me their challenges and most common problems. For one reason or another I couldn't answer them in prior chapters so I decided to cover them all in the final chapter of the book.

Please note that I can't address every possible challenge, but the solution to one problem can often help handle another difficulty. Moreover, many questions and subsequent suggestions are broad enough to cover a lot of related issues.

Due to the number of topics we'll cover in this long chapter, actionable implications will come right after each question instead of at the end of the chapter. Consequently, the final quick recap at the end of the chapter will cover only the most essential points.

Without further ado, let's start.

Q: How Do I Maintain Self-Discipline When Doing Menial or Uncreative Tasks Like Bookkeeping?

Delegation is the answer.

Even the best one-man operation can benefit from delegating some tasks to other people.

It makes little sense to tap into your willpower to force yourself to work on tasks you don't do well like bookkeeping, graphic design, or programming. Doing things you hate will drain you out of energy you could have used on the key tasks. As soon as you can afford it, delegate every single business task that isn't your strength.

If you can't afford to delegate certain tasks, do them all on a day where little happens, like a weekend. This way, they won't occupy your mind during the workweek when you should be focused on the priorities.

Last but not least, if you can't afford to delegate tasks you find boring or annoying, you might as well find some enjoyment in doing them or remind yourself why they're useful.

For instance, for one of my businesses I needed to create a long list of potential customers. It required countless hours of collecting data. I could have grumbled how much I hated it—and for a period of time I did. Then I reminded myself that the spreadsheet I was building was important. I might have not liked collecting data, but the final result—a list of potential customers—would make me money.

Changing my attitude didn't change the fact that I had to do this task, but at least I felt better doing it. It's your choice how your work makes you feel.

Actionable Implications

Figure out which task takes the most of your time or energy and delegate it to someone else. If you still haven't delegated bookkeeping and accounting to a professional, take care of it first. Even if you're a professional bookkeeper or accountant, your job as an entrepreneur is to grow your business, not worry about paperwork.

If you've already delegated these tasks, consider delegating simple time-consuming admin jobs like data entry or jobs you never do well, like graphic design or programming.

If you can't afford to delegate, designate one day a week when you'll take care of all the jobs you hate doing that need to be done.

Lastly, if you can't delegate certain tasks, try to change your attitude about them. You have control over how these tasks make you feel, so find a way to give them some meaning or come up with a way to make them more fun to do.

Q: How Do I Stay Motivated When I Feel Discouraged?

All entrepreneurs constantly have to learn new things and overcome challenges to stay on top of their game. Get used to it; an entrepreneur has to be able to thrive despite difficulties.

To maintain resolve when things get hard and you feel discouraged, prevention—setting the right expectations—is key. Be cautious of the false hope syndrome, a cycle of failure and renewed effort in which people have unrealistic expectations of self-change.[1]

This problem is particularly common among entrepreneurs with little to no business experience who set goals that are almost impossible to achieve.

Don't get me wrong. It's good to think big. However, there's a fine line between thinking big and being unrealistic, and it might be difficult to tell the difference if you don't have much business experience.

Generally speaking, it's good to make peace with the facts that:

1. It's highly unlikely your first business will become wildly successful.

Funders and Founders, a design company specializing in infographics, has created numerous infographics in which they show the paths of the most successful entrepreneurs.[li] One thing you can learn from these infographics is that every entrepreneur needed at least a couple of tries before they achieved big success.

For instance, British billionaire Richard Branson and American billionaire Mark Cuban both started four companies before they made their first million.

When you acknowledge that your first business probably won't be wildly successful, you'll save yourself some disappointment that could otherwise ruin your resolve.

Please note it doesn't mean you should expect your business to bankrupt you. Spectacular failures happen rarely. You're more likely to either lose some money or break even. Don't let a lack of success deter you from starting a company, though. Losing some and winning some is a part of the process to gain experience.

2. It's rare for a young person with little to no work experience to launch a business that will cover all their living expenses within months. It takes years to develop the proper work ethic, mindset, and gain enough knowledge to launch a successful company.

If you're young and inexperienced, come to terms with the fact that your journey will most likely take a few years before you can call yourself a full-time entrepreneur and have the income to prove it.

It took me about seven years to mature as an entrepreneur (and yes, I too deluded myself thinking that it wouldn't take so long). My story isn't rare; most entrepreneurs I know went through a similar process.

Things are brighter for people who possess marketable skills and work ethic developed in a day job. Working for the man may not be what you want, but it's a solid base to transition into entrepreneurship.

According to the *Freelancing in America 2015* report, 60% of the freelancers who left their day jobs now earn more, and of those, 78% indicated that within a year or less they earned more freelancing than in their day job.[lii]

Now, these numbers might not be a 100% representative sample. However, it still shows that it isn't rare for people who already possess the skills to build a successful business, even within a year.

3. Things are supposed to be hard. If they weren't, more people would be successful entrepreneurs. Difficulties are like a rite of passing, and some people transition into entrepreneurship while others are sifted out.

If you start your journey with the assumption it's going to be a piece of cake, you're in for a nasty surprise. I strongly suggest reading at least a few biographies of successful entrepreneurs to understand that gaining early business experience is synonymous with constant challenges and failures.

After setting the right expectations and acknowledging reality, another way to stay motivated when things are hard is to find enjoyment in the process.

When you switch your attitude from "I'll be happy when I make x amount of money with my business" to "I'm grateful to be on this journey, results will soon follow," it will be easier to handle the bad moments. Have your goal in mind, but don't forget to appreciate your current accomplishments, no matter how modest they are.

Last but not least, whenever you find yourself in a difficult situation and your motivation is running out, remind yourself that once you overcome your problems, you'll have a great war story to tell.

One of my businesses landed me in debt. It was hard to stay positive when I was constantly worried about how to keep my business alive *and* get out of debt. What helped me stay motivated was reminding myself that I would eventually handle these problems, and this would make me a stronger person. I would have a great inspirational story to share, too. It sounds trite, but such reminders can make a world of a difference when you feel defeated.

Actionable Implications

Setting the right expectations is key to preventing big disappointments.

Read some real-world stories of successful entrepreneurs to understand the long process needed to make it big. To educate yourself how long it takes for a normal person to achieve success, seek out the stories of average Joes, too. Blogs and forums for entrepreneurs are full of such stories.

If you're already feeling defeated, switch your attitude. Focus on what's right (even if it's a tiny thing) and remind yourself it's a phase, not a permanent situation.

Q: How Do I Maintain Self-Discipline When Everyone Says No?

Everybody who has ever worked in sales knows how debilitating it can be to hear one "no" after another. The more rejections you get, the less motivated you are. How to ensure you won't give up even when everyone says "no"?

1. Give a Monetary Value to a "No"

The worst part about constant rejection is that it feels like you're not going anywhere. And if you're not getting results for a long time, discouragement creeps in. If you've already received some yeses—even just a few—you can guesstimate the ratio of the "yes" and "no" answers and give your "no's" a monetary value.

For instance, if each "yes" means a $100 sale, and you get one "yes" out of one hundred calls, then each rejection "generates" one dollar because it's one "no" closer to a $100 "yes."

Obviously, statistics don't have to work exactly like in this example but it's beside the point. What's important is that giving a "no" a monetary value makes you feel like you're accomplishing something. It's no longer a fruitless undertaking but a process that eventually leads to success.

Remember the words of Thomas Edison: "I have not failed. I've just found 10,000 ways that won't work." Each one of those failures was a valuable investment towards the eventual payoff.

2. Focus on the Action Itself

I used to be an extremely shy person. To overcome my crippling shyness, I forced myself to approach women in the street. As you can probably imagine, most women approached by a stranger will summarily reject him. If I had focused exclusively on the result I would have given up early, embarrassed because of all the rejections.

Consequently, my primary goal wasn't to find a date, but to simply make an approach despite fear. What happened after I uttered the first few words didn't count. However, since I wasn't attached to a particular outcome, I actually did just fine and met with positive reactions.

Once I overcame the fear and became comfortable approaching women, the results came naturally as a byproduct of me focusing on the approach in itself.

I tried the same approach (pardon the pun) in business. Instead of focusing on the end result, I made sure to help a potential client as much as I could. Granted, it's harder not to become attached to a result if you're broke and need to make sales, but it *is* possible. Make an effort to focus on the attempt in itself and helping your potential client. More often than not, it will project a confident aura that will attract them to you.

3. Avoid Hearing "No" Altogether

In many businesses, people rely on brute force marketing techniques. Instead of drawing people in, they push them to buy their products. While this approach can still work in some industries, consumers are increasingly rejecting hard selling. Fewer and fewer people are happy to receive sales calls or emails without asking for them.

Enter permission marketing: a type of marketing where the potential client comes to you instead of the other way around. When was the last time a plastic surgeon called you to try this new plastic surgery of his? Patients seek surgeons, not the other way around.

Position yourself as an expert in your industry or offer some of your products or services for free, and you too can become that surgeon.

I make some of my books and other materials available for free. Potential readers can familiarize themselves with my work with no risk. If they're ready, they can purchase other products. I'm not scouting the Internet, looking for new potential readers and asking them to buy my books. Consequently, I don't have to hear "no's."

Read works by Seth Godin or Perry Marshall's book *80/20 Sales and Marketing* to learn more about how to make people come to you. You'll not only hear "no's" less often, you'll also get better results while working fewer hours.

Actionable Implications

If you have to cold call or cold email potential clients and you've already got a few "yeses," assign a monetary value to each "no." Estimate how many "no's" you need to hear before you get a "yes," calculate the value of an average "yes" and divide it by the number of "no's." There you go, now you know how much each "no" is approximately worth and how close you are to another sale.

In addition to the first technique, you can also switch your attitude to focus on the action itself—like making a call—instead of a particular result. Not having any expectations is often more beneficial than attaching yourself to a particular result (like a sale) and rarely getting it.

Last but not least, if you can't handle the number of "no's" you hear on a daily basis, learn about permission marketing. Think in terms of how you can draw people in instead of chasing them.

Q: How Do I Stay Motivated When All I Can Do Is Wait?

In many businesses you often have to wait for somebody else to deliver your product (your contractor, manufacturer, shipping company), give a green light to release it (your business partner, a government agency, a distributor), or sign a contract to buy your solution (a client).

When there's little you can do to push things forward, you can't be proactive, and this can lead to self-doubt.

There are two primary ways to deal with this issue.

The first one is to get yourself occupied with tasks that might not be particularly important but that need to be done. It might be a perfect time to work on all these menial tasks you couldn't force yourself to do before. Mindless data entry or other admin work might be just what you need to get your mind occupied while you wait for the decision, finished product, or a shipment.

The second way to stay motivated is to shift your mind elsewhere. Since you can't do much during the waiting period anyway, why not use it as an opportunity to take a break or nurture yourself? Find a challenge in sports, learn a new skill, or simply spend some time with your friends and family.

Actionable Implications

If there's little you can do to make things move more quickly, occupy yourself with the little business tasks that should have been done a long time ago but that you always postponed. If you don't have any such tasks, take a break. The key is to take your mind off waiting and do something else.

Q: How Do I Boost My Confidence When Business Goes Down?

Entrepreneurship can be a wild rollercoaster. One day you're on top, the next your heart is in your throat as acceleration pushes you into the seat.

What do you do to deal with low confidence when your business goes down? Or more importantly:

How can you prevent or minimize the discouragement when business slows down?

Here are seven solutions.

1. Have Savings

The less financial security you have, the more of a hit your confidence will take when your business goes down. It's one thing when business goes down but you still have some savings, and another when you can't pay the bills. In the former you can still think clearly, in the latter it's easy to get desperate and make your situation even worse.

Consequently, an emergency fund that will cover at least three to six months of your regular living expenses is a must. If you don't have it yet, start saving a percentage of your income each month to build a fund to support yourself and your family during slower periods.

2. Diagnose and Act

When business goes down, discouragement and resignation may follow. Instead of wallowing in the bad emotions, get your mind off them and diagnose the reason why the business isn't doing well.

Once you make a list of potential reasons, act on them. The mere act of taking action will help you regain control over the situation and recover some self-confidence.

3. Keep Your Eyes Open and Your Lights On

When the business is slow, it's tempting to cut corners. An owner of a brick and mortar store closes it earlier because "nobody will come anyway." An owner of an online business takes longer to reply to potential customers because "after all, what's the difference?"

Such an attitude does nothing to fix the situation. Quite the contrary—it actually worsens it and reduces the chances you'll take advantage of an opportunity when it arises.

Whenever you find yourself in a bad business situation, it's time to up your game. Keep your lights on and your eyes open for possible opportunities to turn the tide.

4. Prioritize Growth Over Cutting Expenses

When you lose confidence in your ability to grow the business, you'll most likely feel the temptation to cut as many expenses as you can. It can be a sound solution only if it's done carefully and to genuine unnecessary expenses.

Unfortunately, many entrepreneurs get too desperate, and instead of finding new ways to increase their revenues they focus almost exclusively on scrimping and saving. As a result, the quality of their products goes down, the morale of their team gets a hit, and the entire business keeps shrinking as "cost optimization" eats it piece by piece.

The only result of prioritizing cost optimization over increasing your profits is that you slow down the decay of the business, but you don't do much to reverse the trend.

To regain control over the bad situation, resist the temptation to cut as many expenses as you can and instead focus on how you can grow your business.

Look at it this way: You can only cut so many expenses, but your earning potential is unlimited.

5. Tweak and Experiment

No matter if things are going well or turning sour, it's vital to invest some of your resources into innovation. Tweaking and experimenting can help you uncover new sources of revenue, trends that you can ride to grow your business, or a new market in which you can become a leader.

When business is slow, it's particularly important to keep trying new things and fixing your existing processes. Getting yourself occupied with improvements will keep your spirits up and provide hope that's essential to stay motivated despite obstacles and setbacks.

6. Get a Fresh Perspective

Bringing a fresh perspective into your business can help you get it back on track.

You don't necessarily have to hire a new employee. A fresh perspective can come from a friend you ask for an opinion, or from professional colleagues on an entrepreneur forum you'll ask for advice. It can also come from you if you go on vacation, recharge your batteries, and come back with new insights and renewed energy to revive your troubled company.

7. Boost your Self-Esteem

As we've already discussed, many entrepreneurs have a tendency to associate their self-esteem with the performance of their business. When the business goes down, your self-esteem takes a hit, too. With low self-esteem, it's harder to maintain your resolve, so it's key to boost your self-esteem as much as you can while you work on your business to get well again.

I strongly suggest having a challenging hobby or two that you can practice to get your mind off business and boost your well-being.

If business is the biggest, or even worse, the *only* factor that defines your self-esteem, a downturn can wreak havoc on your levels of self-discipline. If many things contribute to your sense of esteem, it will be more crisis-resistant.

Actionable Implication

I've just given you seven practical ways to deal with low self-confidence when your business goes down. The bottom line—and ultimately the most important actionable implication you can get out of this subchapter—is that when your business goes down, it's time to get even more proactive. If you drop guard, you'll get hit even harder.

If you're now in such a situation, get yourself together, set a timer for thirty minutes and make a list of actions you can take to help your business stand on firm ground again.

It doesn't matter if your business is suffering because of an economic downturn or anything else you can't control. There's always something you can do to fix the situation, and it's always better than resignation.

Q: How Do I Beat Short-Term Attacks of Procrastination?

You sit in front of your computer and look at your to-do list. You know what needs to be done, but for some reason you can't fathom, you just can't.

Short-term attacks of procrastination are different than long-term procrastination. With the latter, you postpone things for days or weeks on end. While you can eliminate this kind of procrastination from your life almost entirely, dealing with short-term intensive bursts of inertia isn't that feasible. Such days just sometimes happen.

Instead of trying to get motivated, what usually helps me is to try to get *momentum*.

When I asked a bestselling author and fitness expert Derek Doepker what was his top strategy for persistence, he replied, "I simply ask myself, 'Can I just…?' and then insert an action so easy I can do it no matter how unmotivated I feel.

"Have you ever noticed that it's *after* you start doing something, *then* you feel like you want to keep on going? Instead of trying to get motivation, try to get momentum. The motivation will naturally follow. Success breeds success. Each time you're victorious at doing even a little thing, your sense of accomplishment and desire to do more will grow."[liii]

In fact, I used this little trick right before writing these words. I struggled to motivate myself to start writing, so I started putting some words on the page. An hour has passed and my daily word quota has been accomplished, almost as if by magic.

Actionable Implication

Whatever your task is, get started on it—not with the intention to finish it, but just to get momentum. More often than not, taking the first steps is all that's needed to overcome procrastination and regain motivation.

Q: How Do I Find the Willpower to Work on My Business If I Have a Day Job and Other Obligations?

Working on your business is hard enough, and it's even harder with a day job and other obligations. Now, don't get me wrong—it's not a viable excuse. A lot of people have been in the exact same situation and figured it out. You can do it, too.

I could give you numerous tips how to make more time during your day (I cover a lot of them in my book *How to Have More Time*), but in the end there's only one extremely effective piece of advice you should definitely implement in your life: the one-hour workday.

Before you call me crazy thinking I must have surely lost my bearings, please hear me out. We all like to believe we're working extremely hard and there's absolutely not enough time to fit everything into the busy schedule. In reality, the problem isn't about not having enough time as about not having enough *distraction-free* time.

You'd be surprised how much you could achieve if you only spend sixty minutes working in a truly focused way with *zero* distractions.

I put so much emphasis throughout the book on the fact that building your business should be first and foremost sustainable because it's the key to productivity. Don't fall victim to the glamorous hundred-hour workweek which perhaps makes you look like a hero but in the end leads to decreased productivity, burnout, exhaustion, sickness, or in the worst cases, even death (*karōshi* or "overwork death" is a real threat in Japan[liv]).

Jeffrey J. McDonnell, a professor in the School of Environment and Sustainability at the University of Saskatchewan in Saskatoon, Canada, wrote an article titled "The One-Hour Workday" in which he praises the power of doing small amounts of focused writing every day.[lv]

As McDonnell points out in the article, despite him working like a madman, his productivity as measured by paper output was meager. It was only when he introduced a one-hour workday—one hour of focused writing every single morning—that he could finally get something done.

My one-hour workday is similar. If I'm writing a new book, it's writing one thousand words a day. If I'm editing a book, it's editing a chapter a day. Even if I don't accomplish anything else, it's still a productive day.

What is your one-hour workday? Figure out one key task that will help you grow your business and focus on it during your magic hour. If you stick to such a routine every single day—and one hour a day is manageable, isn't it?—the results will amaze you.

The key to make this strategy work is to find at least one hour of distraction-free time. I strongly suggest waking up early—5:00 or 6:00 AM—for the quietest time during the day.

Even if you consider yourself a night owl, I still urge you to experiment with early rising. I used to stay up until 3:00 AM. Now I regularly wake up at 5:00 AM and am done with all key tasks (daily hygiene, exercise, work) before 9:00 AM.

Actionable Implication

Right now, set your alarm clock at least one hour earlier than usual. Starting tomorrow, protect the first hour of your day as the most sacrosanct time in your life.

Spend the entire hour working on the most important task that will push your business forward. Even if you can't afford to spend more time working on your business, it will still get you closer to reaching your goal than you imagine.

FREQUENTLY ASKED QUESTIONS RELATED TO SELF-DISCIPLINE: QUICK RECAP

1. If you find it hard to maintain self-discipline when you're working on menial tasks, find a way to delegate them. If you can't do it, batch them and do them during one day. Changing your attitude about these tasks—finding meaning and usefulness in them instead of complaining how boring and uncreative they are—will also help you.

2. It's easy to lose motivation when things are hard and it seems like you'll never achieve your goals. The key to keeping your spirits up is to have the right expectations. For example, research how often it takes a regular person to achieve the goal you want to achieve instead of assuming you can do it unrealistically quickly.

Also, don't forget that it's the process that makes you successful. Appreciate it for all it brings into your life, including challenges.

3. Hearing "no's" all the time can break the resolve of even the most disciplined person. The best

way to deal with rejection is to focus on the action itself and stop attaching yourself to the result.

4. If you find yourself in a situation where all you can do is wait, get yourself occupied with tasks that you've been procrastinating on for a long time. Obsessing over the fact that you'll have to wait can lead to self-doubt and discouragement. Alternatively, take advantage of the opportunity to take a quick break and return with renewed energy.

5. The key to dealing with a negative emotional state when your business goes down is to stay proactive. If you let resignation take control over your life, you might as well give up now. Take an action—any action—to get yourself out of the hole instead of digging an even deeper one.

6. If you find it hard to get started on your everyday tasks, try to start working with no expectation of finishing a given activity. Just write the first sentence, email one client, write the first line of code, or whatever it takes to begin work. More often than not, within minutes you'll gain momentum to keep going.

7. A day job and other obligations can make it hard to work on your business. It doesn't mean it's a good excuse not to stay self-disciplined, though. Use the power of the "one-hour workday" to ensure steady—even if slow—progress. Wake up early and dedicate the entire sixty minutes to distraction-free work on the most important task. Even if it's all you can do to grow your business on a daily basis, one focused hour of work a day can bring extraordinary results.

Epilogue

I believe that entrepreneurs are the lifeblood of our modern world and they need all the support they can get. I wrote this book to add my small contribution and help you gain practical knowledge to improve your self-discipline and make your life as an entrepreneur easier.

The life of an entrepreneur can be arduous, but its rewards are worth it. Few lifestyle choices can provide you with so many enriching experiences as building your own business. Likewise, nothing else will test your persistence and self-discipline as much as being out there on your own, being the only person responsible for your success.

As a final quick recap, I want you to remember that:

- It all starts with proper motivation. If you're an entrepreneur by nature, you most likely won't lack a solid reason why you should keep going, but it's still worth it to consider various additional motivators to strengthen your resolve.

- Your surroundings create your life. It's your choice who your friends are, what books you read, how you spend your time, and what behaviors you exhibit on a daily basis.

- Make your life about more than just entrepreneurship. It's addictive to work on your business, but it shouldn't be the only love of your life. Remember that you work to live, not live to work.

- Dedication and focus are the keys to success. In our rapidly moving world it's harder and harder to maintain single focus and commit, but you aren't an entrepreneur because you want to be like everybody else, right?

- Being proactive is vital to develop a proper attitude. Entrepreneurs don't *wait* for things to happen, they *make* them happen.

I want you to keep creating new things, starting new ventures or improving your existing businesses, and changing the world for the better with your unique entrepreneurial energy and spirit.

Keep going despite whatever life throws at you, say "no" to things that endanger your long-term results, and strive to improve your self-discipline. It's only by maintaining a strong work ethic and being comfortable with discomfort you can continuously achieve more and more in both your entrepreneurial and personal life.

I hope we'll see each other in my other books in which you'll learn about improving other aspects of your life and achieving ultimate success. Good luck!

Download Another Book for Free

I want to thank you for buying my book and offer you another book (just as valuable as this book): *Grit: How to Keep Going When You Want to Give Up*, completely free.

Visit the link below to receive it:

http://www.profoundselfimprovement.com/selfdisciplineforentrepreneurs

In *Grit*, I'll share with you exactly how to stick to your goals according to peak performers and scientific evidence.

In addition to getting *Grit*, you'll also have an opportunity to get my new books for free, enter giveaways, and receive other valuable emails from me.

Again, here's the link to sign up:

http://www.profoundselfimprovement.com/selfdisciplineforentrepreneurs

Could You Help?

I'd love to hear your opinion about my book. In the world of book publishing, there are few things more valuable than honest reviews from a wide variety of readers.

Your review will help other readers find out whether my book is for them. It will also help me reach more readers by increasing the visibility of my book.

About Martin Meadows

Martin Meadows is the pen name of an author who has dedicated his life to personal growth. He constantly reinvents himself by making drastic changes in his life.

Over the years, he has regularly fasted for over forty hours, taught himself two foreign languages, lost over thirty pounds in twelve weeks, ran several businesses in various industries, taken ice-cold showers and baths, lived on a small tropical island in a foreign country for several months, and has written a 400-page long novel's worth of short stories in one month.

Yet self-torture is not his passion. Martin likes to test his boundaries to discover how far his comfort zone goes.

His findings (based both on his personal experience and scientific studies) help him improve his life. If you're interested in pushing your limits and learning how to become the best version of yourself, you'll love Martin's works.

You can read his books here:

http://www.amazon.com/author/martinmeadows.

[i] Ryan, R. M., & Deci, E. L. (2000). Intrinsic and Extrinsic Motivations: Classic Definitions and New Directions. *Contemporary Educational Psychology*, 25(1), 54-67. doi: 10.1006/ceps.1999.1020

[ii] Ryan, R. M., & Deci, E. L. (2000). Intrinsic and Extrinsic Motivations: Classic Definitions and New Directions. *Contemporary Educational Psychology*, 25(1), 54-67. doi: 10.1006/ceps.1999.1020

[iii] Preston, J. (2014, August 26). Richard Branson: My golden rule of business. Retrieved July 26, 2016, from https://www.virgin.com/entrepreneur/richard-branson-my-golden-rule-of-business

[iv] Harris, P. (2010, August 1). Elon Musk: 'I'm planning to retire to Mars'. Retrieved July 26, 2016, from https://www.theguardian.com/technology/2010/aug/01/elon-musk-spacex-rocket-mars

[v] Waters, R. (2005, December 22). Google's founders named Men of the Year. Retrieved July 26, 2016 from http://www.ft.com/cms/s/2/86e14656-7315-11da-8b42-0000779e2340.html#axzz4FXl8Ba1e

[vi] Tang, S., & Hall, V. C. (1995). The overjustification effect: A meta-analysis. *Applied Cognitive Psychology*, 9(5), 365-404. doi: 10.1002/acp.2350090502

[vii] Silver, Y. (2015). *Evolved Enterprise: How to Re-think, Re-imagine, and Re-invent Your Business to Deliver Meaningful Impact & Even Greater Profits*. Retrieved from https://evolvedenterprise.com/

[viii] Grant, A. M. (2008). Does Intrinsic Motivation Fuel the Prosocial Fire? Motivational Synergy in Predicting Persistence, Performance, and Productivity. *Journal of Applied Psychology*, 93(1): 48-58. doi: 0.1037/0021-9010.93.1.48

[ix] About Sevenly. Retrieved July 27, 2016 from https://www.sevenly.org/pages/about-us

[x] Kahneman, D., & Deaton, A. (2010). High income improves evaluation of life but not emotional well-being. *Proceedings of*

the National Academy of Sciences, 107(38): 16489-16493. doi: 10.1073/pnas.1011492107

[xi] Bandura, A. (1977). *Social Learning Theory*. Englewood Cliffs, NJ: Prentice-Hall.

[xii] *Anderson, C. A., & Bushman, B. J. (2001). Effects of violent video games on aggressive behavior, aggressive cognition, aggressive affect, physiological arousal, and pro-social behavior: A meta-analytic review of the scientific literature. Psychological Science, 12(5): 353-359. doi:10.1111/1467-9280.00366*

[xiii] Paik, H., & Comstock, G. (1994). The effects of television violence on antisocial behavior: A meta-analysis. *Communication Research*, 21(4): 516-546. doi:10.1177/009365094021004004

[xiv] Baumeister, R. F. (2003). Ego Depletion and Self-Regulation Failure: A Resource Model of Self-Control. *Alcoholism: Clinical & Experimental Research*, 27(2): 281-284. doi: 10.1097/01.ALC.0000060879.61384.A4

[xv] Ferriss, T. (2009). *The 4-Hour Workweek: Escape 9-5, Live Anywhere, and Join the New Rich.* New York: Crown Publishers.

[xvi] Johnston, W. M., & Davey, G. C. L. (1997). The psychological impact of negative TV news bulletins: The catastrophizing of personal worries. *British Journal of Psychology*, 88(1): 85-91. doi: 10.1111/j.2044-8295.1997.tb02622.x

[xvii] Schwartz, M. (2007, March 7). Robert Sapolsky discusses physiological effects of stress. Retrieved July 29, 2016 from http://news.stanford.edu/news/2007/march7/sapolskysr-030707.html

[xviii] Brown, L. (2016, August 20). Refuse to complain. Complaining is just a way of not taking responsibility, justifying doing nothing, and programming yourself to fail [Facebook status update]. Retrieved August 21, 2016, from https://www.facebook.com/Brown.Les/posts/101543774388496 54

[xix] Grant, A. M. (2013). *Give and Take: Why Helping Others Drives Our Success*. New York, NY: Viking.

[xx] McKinney, F. (2002). *Make It Big: 49 Secrets for Building a Life of Extreme Success*. New York, NY: John Wiley & Sons.

[xxi] Burg, B., & Mann, J. D. (2007). *The Go-Giver, Expanded Edition: A Little Story About a Powerful Business Idea*. New York, NY: Portfolio.

[xxii] Bartolotta, D. L. (1998). If At First You Don't Succeed... What Makes You Try Again? Retrieved July 29 from http://repository.cmu.edu/cgi/viewcontent.cgi?article=1033&context=hsshonors

[xxiii] Christy, M. (1982, May 9). Winning according to Schwarzenegger. *Boston Globe*. p. 51.

[xxiv] McGonigal, K. (2012). *The Willpower Instinct: How Self-Control Works, Why It Matters, and What You Can Do to Get More of It*. New York, NY: Avery.

[xxv] Baumeister, R. F. (2003). Ego Depletion and Self-Regulation Failure: A Resource Model of Self-Control. *Alcoholism: Clinical & Experimental Research*, 27(2): 281-284. doi: 10.1097/01.ALC.0000060879.61384.A4

[xxvi] Williamson, A., & Feyer, A. (2000). Moderate sleep deprivation produces impairments in cognitive and motor performance equivalent to legally prescribed levels of alcohol intoxication. *Occupational & Environmental Medicine*, 57(10): 649-655. doi: 10.1136/oem.57.10.649

[xxvii] Simmons, M. (2013, May 13). Is The 70-Hour Work Week Worth The Sacrifice? Retrieved July 30, 2016, from http://www.forbes.com/sites/michaelsimmons/2013/05/13/is-the-70-hour-work-week-worth-the-sacrifice/

[xxviii] DeMarco, M. J (2011). *The Millionaire Fastlane: Crack the Code to Wealth and Live Rich for a Lifetime*. Phoenix, AZ: Viperion Publishing Corporation.

[xxix] King, S. (2010). *On Writing: 10th Anniversary Edition: A Memoir of the Craft*. New York, NY: Scribner.

[xxx] Holiday, R. (2016). *Ego Is the Enemy*. New York, NY: Portfolio.

[xxxi] Rock, D. (2009). *Your Brain at Work: Strategies for Overcoming Distraction, Regaining Focus, and Working Smarter All Day Long*. New York, NY: HarperCollins.

[xxxii] Rock, D. (2009, October 04). Easily distracted: Why it's hard to focus, and what to do about it. Retrieved August 06, 2016, from https://www.psychologytoday.com/blog/your-brain-work/200910/easily-distracted-why-its-hard-focus-and-what-do-about-it

[xxxiii] Pattison, K. (2008, July 28). Worker, Interrupted: The Cost of Task Switching. Retrieved August 06, 2016, from http://www.fastcompany.com/944128/worker-interrupted-cost-task-switching.

[xxxiv] The Pomodoro Technique. Retrieved August 06, 2016 from http://pomodorotechnique.com/

[xxxv] K. D. Vohs, R., Baumeister, J. M., Twinge, B. J., Schmeichel, D. M., Tice, & J., Crocker (2005). *Decision fatigue exhausts self-regulatory resources--but so does accommodating to unchosen alternatives*. Retrieved August 7, 2016 from https://www.chicagobooth.edu/research/workshops/marketing/archive/WorkshopPapers/vohs.pdf

[xxxvi] Anderson, C. (2003). The Psychology of Doing Nothing: Forms of Decision Avoidance Result from Reason and Emotion. *Psychological Bulletin*, 129(1): 139-167. doi: 10.1037/0033-2909.129.1.139

[xxxvii] Baer, D. (2014, February 12). Always Wear The Same Suit: Obama's Presidential Productivity Secrets. Retrieved August 10, 2016, from http://www.fastcompany.com/3026265/work-smart/always-wear-the-same-suit-obamas-presidential-productivity-secrets

[xxxviii] Kirby, L. D., Morrow, J., & Yih, J. (2014). *The challenge of challenge: Pursuing determination as an emotion*. In M. M., Tugade, M. N., Shiota, & L. D., Kirby (Eds.), *Handbook of Positive Emotions*. New York, NY: Guilford Publications.

[xxxix] Rotter, J. B. (1966). Generalized expectancies for internal versus external control of reinforcement. Psychological

175

Monographs: General & Applied, 80(1): 1-28. doi: 10.1037/h0092976

[xl] Bandura, A. (1994). *Self-efficacy*. In V. S., Ramachaudran (Ed.), *Encyclopedia of human behavior*, vol. 4, pp. 71-81. Cambridge, MA: Academic Press.

[xli] Carnegie Mellon University (2007, December 20) *Randy Pausch Last Lecture: Achieving Your Childhood Dreams* [Video file]. Retrieved August 7, 2016 from https://www.youtube.com/watch?v=ji5_MqicxSo

[xlii] *Wantrepreneur*. Urban Dictionary. Retrieved August 16, from http://www.urbandictionary.com/define.php?term=wantrepreneu r

[xliii] Williams, B. (2006, May 25). Steve Jobs: Iconoclast and salesman. Retrieved August 17, 2016, from http://www.nbcnews.com/id/12974884/

[xliv] Van Boven, L., & Gilovich, T. (2003). To Do or to Have? That Is the Question. *Journal of Personality and Social Psychology*, 85(6): 1193-1202. doi: 10.1037/0022-3514.85.6.1193

[xlv] Van Boven, L. (2005). Experientialism, Materialism, and the Pursuit of Happiness. *Review of General Psychology*, 9(2): 132-142. doi: 10.1037/1089-2680.9.2.132

[xlvi] Kumar, A., Killingsworth, M. A., & Gilovich, T. (2014). Waiting for Merlot. Anticipatory Consumption of Experiential and Material Purchases. *Psychological Science*, 25(10): 1924-1931. doi: 10.1177/0956797614546556

[xlvii] Pchelin, P., & Howell, R. T. (2014). The hidden cost of value-seeking: People do not accurately forecast the economic benefits of experiential purchases. *The Journal of Positive Psychology*, 9(4): 322-334. doi: 10.1080/17439760.2014.898316

[xlviii] Patel, N. (2015, April 02). *Why You Should Never Start Just One Business*. Retrieved August 18, 2016, from https://www.entrepreneur.com/article/244560

[xlix] Sivers, D. (2016, August 02). *When you're extremely un-motivated*. Retrieved August 18, 2016, from https://sivers.org/unmo

[l] Polivy, J. (2001). The false hope syndrome: unrealistic expectations of self-change. *International Journal of Obesity and Related Metabolic Disorders*, 25 Suppl 1: S80-4. doi: 10.1038/sj.ijo.0801705

[li] Vital, A. (2013, August 23). *Serial Entrepreneurs – The Founders Who Pursue Multiple Opportunities*. Retrieved August 23, 2016 from http://fundersandfounders.com/serial-entrepreneurs-how-to-pursue-multiple-opportunities/

[lii] *Freelancing in America: 2015*. Retrieved August 23, 2016, from https://fu-web-storage-prod.s3.amazonaws.com/content/filer_public/59/e7/59e70be1-5730-4db8-919f-1d9b5024f939/survey_2015.pdf

[liii] Meadows, M. (2015). *Grit: How to Keep Going When You Want to Give Up*. Retrieved from http://www.amazon.com/dp/B00V60LU20.

[liv] *Karōshi*. (2016, August 2). In Wikipedia, The Free Encyclopedia. Retrieved August 22, 2016, from https://en.wikipedia.org/w/index.php?title=Kar%C5%8Dshi&oldid=732672121

[lv] McDonnell, J. (2016). The 1-hour workday. *Science*, 353(6300), 718. doi: 10.1126/science.353.6300.718.

Made in the USA
Middletown, DE
07 October 2017